To the Greatest Grandpa.

We sure love you.

Love

Jim & Judy
Steve, Joe, Ken
+ Kristi
Christmas 86

SERMONS *not* SPOKEN

SERMONS
not
SPOKEN
NEAL A. MAXWELL

BOOKCRAFT
Salt Lake City, Utah

Library of Congress Catalog Card Number: 85-72078
ISBN 0-88494-571-5

First Printing, 1985

Printed in the United States of America

Contents

Preface

Duties and ponderings have occasionally stirred the author to prepare drafts of sermons which, for one reason or another, were not spoken; or perhaps only small portions were extracted and used. Other times, a talk has been prepared for which there was neither occasion nor audience.

Whether the author simply needed the spiritual calisthenics which go with such added preparation, it now matters not. These "Sermons Not Spoken" are here printed for audiences unseen, but with no less desire that somehow, for them, they will prove helpful.

As always, it should be said that this is *not* an official Church publication. The views expressed herein are those for which the author alone is solely responsible.

Genuine appreciation is expressed to Daniel H. Ludlow and Roy W. Doxey for their review of and suggestions concerning this manuscript and to Susan Jackson for processing, so patiently, the flow of words.

"Enlarged the Memory of This People"

(Alma 37:8)

So far as our Christian convictions are concerned, individuals are almost never more than one generation away from regression, dissension, or disaffection! The last-named can happen very quickly, as in this instance centuries ago.

> And there arose another generation after them, which knew not the Lord, nor yet the works which he had done for Israel (Judges 2:10).

If parents will not commit fully, they cannot transmit fully; then the rising generation, all too soon, in the intriguing words of Nephi, becomes "for themselves" (3 Nephi 1:29). Usually, therefore, spiritual impressions are most deeply made when the "tablets of memory are soft" . . . especially in a hardening, secular age such as this.

The transmitting is best done by a triad consisting

of righteous parents, the Holy Ghost, and the holy
scriptures. The scriptures constitute our collective
memory without which so many have "suffered in
ignorance" (Mosiah 1:3). Used effectively, the scriptures, as was done anciently, can actually enlarge "the
memory of this people," emancipating them, in a
sense, from the limitations of their own time (see Alma
37:8). The enlargement includes conveying the experiences of others which the current generation has not
had, and in such a way as to permit its members to con-
ceptualize, appreciate, and learn from these experiences.

Even when the Holy Ghost teaches us, He too relies
much on human memory. John Donne said that, "the
Holy-Ghost takes the neerest way to bring a man to
God, by awaking his memory," since "memory is
oftener the Holy Ghosts Pulpit." (Janel M. Mueller, ed.,
Donne's Prebend Sermons [Harvard University Press,
1971], p. 33.)

In this matter of transmitting, spiritual history
shows that after all we can do, we should not be sur-
prised when responses to Christ's gospel vary.

Members of the same rising generation, as in earlier
circumstances, may even receive "the same instruction
and the same information" (Alma 47:36), yet some
believe and others dissent. Clearly, each individual and
each rising generation is left free to choose (see 2 Nephi
2:27; 10:23). But it should be an informed choice,
informed especially in those three ways just described
—conceptualization, appreciation, and learning.

Youth may even have gifts, including the gift of the
Holy Ghost, and yet be like counterparts of old who
"knew it not" (3 Nephi 9:20). Concerning the gospel
message, they may be like busy and preoccupied
Amulek: "I knew concerning these things, yet I would
not know" (Alma 10:6).

Hence the urgency of our coming to know God and His scheme of things, and of also developing within ourselves, our children, and our grandchildren a sense of history, including what God has done for Israel. Such reminders of the past—and millennia of memories from the scriptures—will help us amid present challenges.

For instance, one religious and political leader, Shez, had the difficult assignment of beginning "to build up again a broken people" (Ether 10:1). To begin with, Shez remembered "the destruction of his fathers" and also "remembered what the Lord had done in bringing Jared and his brother across the deep." This sense of spiritual history helped him as he began to "build up a righteous kingdom" of people who, once again, learned to "walk in the ways of the Lord" (Ether 10:2).

This "memory" or sense of history should reach back not just a few decades but to the very beginning —even way back to the stated purposes of the Lord with regard to this whole mortal experience. There are, for instance, certain scriptures which, as John Donne observed of certain "imperial psalms," "spread themselves over all occasions." Certain scriptures, such as the following, are so linked to the purposes of God's plan of salvation and this life that they "spread themselves over all occasions."

> And we will prove them *herewith,* to see if they will do all things whatsoever the Lord their God shall command them (Abraham 3:25; italics added).

> For he will give unto the faithful line upon line, precept upon precept; and . . . try you and prove you *herewith* (D&C 98:12; italics added).

The word *herewith* means "in this way" or "in this manner." Such imperial scriptures give us a framework for better understanding mortality amid "all occasions."

Equipped with such a framework, along with a sense of history, we find that a great many things become clearer.

This sense of spiritual history will thus truly help Church members to stay the course, to hold out faithful, and to endure well (see D&C 6:13; D&C 121:8). And surely some such guide and stay is crucial to us, for it will take both testimony and spiritual sophistication to ride out some of the challenges of our time and to avoid being diverted or discouraged.

Suppose, for instance, Church members today were to be asked to pass through a spiritual—not military—equivalent of the "Gideon Scenario." On that occasion 32,000 warriors were rejected in favor of only 300 to be led to victory by Gideon. Why? So that when they triumphed, Israel would know that the Lord—not they—had wrought the victory! Therefore, Israel could not "vaunt themselves." (See Judges 7:2, 7, 16–23.) Ease and self-sufficiency leave no room for meekness and spiritual submissiveness. Hence we too must come to know that events and circumstances may sometimes converge to teach us lessons which we must learn, lest we "vaunt" ourselves.

Not only do the scriptures constitute the moral memory of mankind, but in their precious pages the doctrines of the Church are carefully and deliberately balanced. These doctrines of the kingdom need each other much as the people of the Church need each other. Gospel principles are so powerful that it is not good for them to be alone, either. When "fitly framed" together, they produce conceptual and behavioral balance. But when one of them is isolated from the others, it may go either limp or wild.

It is not just mercy and justice which are to be balanced. In the ecology of God, all His truths and commandments are principles in perpetual partnership. Together, they can produce human happiness here and salvation and exaltation in the world to come.

As the scriptures thus enlarge our memory, they give us enhanced appreciation not only of the prophetic messages but also of the messengers themselves—their humanity, their triumphs, and their differing personalities—as in the following examples.

Once some earlier Church leaders spoke with an unadmired Galilean accent (see Mark 14:70). John the Baptist, than whom there was no greater prophet, had a diet that included locusts but not soufflés, wild honey but not chocolate mousse. Peter and John were viewed by the sophisticates in Jerusalem's power structure as "unlearned and ignorant" (Acts 4:13).

Articulate and educated Paul, on the other hand, was chided because "much learning doth make thee mad" (Acts 26:24). It was further said of Paul, "His letters . . . are weighty and powerful, but his bodily presence is weak, and his speech contemptible" (2 Corinthians 10:10).

Throughout scriptural history, we thus see recurring efforts to demean prophets in order to dismiss them—to label them in order to diminish them. After all, the early Christians were merely "the sect of the Nazarenes" (Acts 24:5)!

Unsurprisingly, therefore, Joseph Smith reflected some of the anxieties and activities of his time and period. Yet a torrent of truth came through that brilliant, good, but imperfect conduit, almost more than Joseph could communicate:

> It is my meditation all the day and more than my
> meat and drink to know how I shall make the saints

of God to comprehend the visions that roll like an
overflowing surge, before my mind (Andrew F. Ehat
and Lyndon W. Cook, comp., *The Words of Joseph
Smith* [BYU Religious Studies Center, 1980], p. 196).

Just a few scant days before his martyrdom, Joseph
affirmed:

> I never told you I was perfect; but there is no error
> in the revelations which I have taught. Must I, then,
> be thrown away as a thing of naught? (*Teachings of
> the Prophet Joseph Smith,* p. 368.)

There is no error in the revelations Joseph taught!

In addition to memory enlargement and increased
appreciation for the prophets, another important
reason for us to be deeply and constantly involved
with the holy scriptures is to receive spiritual refresh-
ment, lest, as feared by Paul, we might "be wearied
and faint in [our] minds" (Hebrews 12:3).

We usually think of weariness as being physical,
but there is also a weariness of mind. When we sing
about knowing that our "Redeemer lives," each of us
pleads that the Lord will "comfort me when faint."
The Holy Ghost can comfort us and so can the holy
scriptures.

By deriving nourishment from the scriptures, we
can be freshened in our minds and hearts. If, as Alma
urged, we are in the continuous process of personal
verification of gospel principles, moving from a mere
desire to believe, to belief, to faith, and even to spiritual knowledge . . . all this will keep us intellectually
and spiritually vibrant (see Alma 32:34).

Brigham Young made the same promise as Alma:

> Every principle God has revealed carries its own
> convictions of its truth to the human mind (Brigham
> Young, *Journal of Discourses* 9:149).

Unsurprisingly, Jesus said the same thing:

If any man will do his will, he *shall know* of the doctrine, whether it be of God, or whether I speak of myself (John 7:17; italics added).

Ponder the fact that Jesus used the words "shall know."

Thus the interplay of scripture and memory freshens us, causing us to be intellectually honest with regard to spiritual knowledge previously obtained, a blessed combination of memory and honesty. Do we not sing as we thank God for a prophet that, as to our God, "We've proved Him in days that are past"?

One cannot study the scriptures long, then, without developing a special appreciation for those scriptures which "spread themselves over all occasions." These scriptures and their companions need to be pondered regularly because they are sobering reminders not only of the framework of this mortal experience—the purposes of life and the frame of reference within which we are to live out our lives—but also of its very center: Heavenly Father's plan of salvation, the atonement of His Son Jesus Christ, and the manner in which we should cope with the tutoring experience of mortal life.

Nevertheless the Lord seeth fit to chasten his people; yea, he trieth their patience and their faith (Mosiah 23:21; see also James 1:3).

For the natural man . . . becometh a saint through the atonement of Christ the Lord, and becometh as a child, submissive, meek, humble, patient, full of love, willing to submit to all things which the Lord seeth fit to inflict upon him, even as a child doth submit to his father (Mosiah 3:19).

And always the needed reassurance is there, as stated in another imperial scripture:

> Who shall separate us from the love of Christ? shall tribulation, or distress, or persecution, or famine, or nakedness, or peril, or sword? (Romans 8:35.)

Relative to those words of Paul's, just because the Lord who thus loves us chooses to protect the faithful for His purposes on one occasion, this does not necessarily mean He will on another. It is a matter of attuning our hearts to scriptures, such as the above. These pertain daily and directly to our trust in God to the point of spiritual submissiveness. If the test comes, we must be like the about-to-be-burned Abinadi, who desired to finish his message "and then it matters not" (Mosiah 13:9); or the three young men, Shadrach, Meshach, and Abed-nego, who said it all in three brave and brief words:

> If it be so, our God whom we serve is able to deliver us from the burning fiery furnace, and he will deliver us out of thine hand, O king.
> *But if not,* be it known unto thee, O king, that we will not serve thy gods, nor worship the golden image which thou hast set up. (Daniel 3:17, 18, italics added; see also Mosiah 13:9 for a comparable "it matters not" statement.)

The same spiritual submissiveness as in these faith-filled three words "but if not" was demonstrated by a young woman in response to an angelic messenger's tidings. The marvelous, spiritually submissive Mary likewise expressed it in few words. Though filled with wonderment about the miraculous impending birth of Jesus, she said, "Behold the handmaid of the Lord; be it unto me according to thy word" (Luke 1:38).

Her words can guide us when we too are puzzled by what is impending or unfolding in our lives. When we cannot explain all that is happening to us or around us, we can adopt Nephi's position:

> I know that [God] loveth his children; nevertheless,
> I do not know the meaning of all things (1 Nephi
> 11:17).

As God enlarges our memories, so to speak, as we "give place" in our lives for the light and warmth of the holy scriptures, not only the periphery of our perspective but also the foundations of our faith are similarly enlarged. Nephi's trust in God was enlarged by Nephi's study of the scriptures—including the words of Isaiah, of which he had surely been aware even before obtaining the plates of Laban. Jesus Himself said, "Great are the words of Isaiah" (3 Nephi 23:1). Isaiah's faith was great, and it in turn enlarged the faith of Nephi, as reading of Nephi's faith can enlarge our faith.

The greater the circumference of our collective spirituality, the larger the pulpit of memory from which the Holy Ghost can stir us. We are far more likely to "come off conqueror" in our holy present if we are truly familiar with mankind's spiritual past.

The Cares of the World
(Luke 8:14)

We must never underestimate the erosive power of routine and repetition insofar as the cares of the world are concerned. There are, depending upon one's particular cluster of cares, different things to be guarded against. Regardless of role, the challenge is there for us all.

The businessman, with his understandable concern for "the bottom line," must ever be reminded that the economic bottom line is not really life's bottom line. But the competing nature of business and the striving of peers for ascendancy can blur the vision of even a good person. In fact, the demanding and consuming cares of the world can even come to endow selfishness with artificial legitimacy. Likewise, such cares bring their own brief satisfactions:

> But if it be not built upon my gospel, and is built upon the works of men, or upon the works of the

devil, verily I say unto you they have *joy in their works for a season,* and by and by the end cometh, and they are hewn down and cast into the fire, from whence there is no return (3 Nephi 27:11; italics added).

For the academician in his search for truth and in his efforts for its preservation or dissemination, the admiration and esteem of his peers is both useful and desirable. But these too can be easily corrupted into an inordinate desire for "the praise of men." Sophistry can come to be preferred to simplicity. The language of scholarship, necessary in its realm, can come to be preferred to the language of faith. Once again, even for the person of faith, the incessant requirements of such associations can come to cloud one's perspective.

For the person involved in government or politics, the constant striving for preeminence or the challenge over turf can get in the way of giving service to others. Some civil servants are barely civil. For some politicians, "getting even" is, somehow, seen as succeeding. Nor are "protective dog-in-the-manger" types likely to give place and priority to Him who was placed in a manger after His birth!

Though Pilate found no fault with Jesus, Pilate still yielded to the mob, and—of momentary significance —he apparently realized some political gain:

> And the same day Pilate and Herod were made friends together: for before they were at enmity between themselves (Luke 23:12).

Victory at the polls, winning at a hearing, and dominating the news, even though only over some passing concern, can easily seem to constitute the whole of life. Moreover, reinforcement by the media (with their fascination with sensation and preference for information instead of wisdom) only intensifies the illusion. The world may, for instance, confer dazzling publicity upon those who swear falsely against the Lord's servants, but it lasts only for a season, after which such critics are "despised by those that flattered them" (D&C 121:20).

No wonder William Wordsworth, anchored in ample observations of his own, gave us those marvelous lines: "The world is too much with us: late and soon, / Getting and spending, we lay waste our powers." (John Bartlett, *Bartlett's Familiar Quotations* [London: MacMillan, 1968], p. 515.)

The challenge of such cares of the world was always real enough, even in the so-called Christian world in decades past. Today, though, these worldly cares comprise particularly profound challenges in a secular setting: they make no apologetic intrusion, but instead present themselves as if they were all of life itself.

For one reason, it is unfashionable to be spiritual. A genius possessed of religious faith is sometimes tolerated among colleagues in the business, academic, or political world. His bilingual ability to converse in the language of his professional realm and in the realm of faith is noted but not often applauded.

Unsurprisingly, when life is seen solely by the natural eye and not at all by the eye of faith, the framework for living is, at once, shifted markedly, if not irrevocably. And the natural eye is so naturally attuned for viewing the cares of the world.

It is useful at times, therefore, for the Christian beset with the cares of the world to be reminded of some of those good individuals who have lost that precious perspective of faith for a season.

What of that mess of pottage now, for which Esau was willing to sell his birthright? (See Genesis 25:29–34.) Not understanding his birthright, Esau "despised" it. Later he despised Jacob too, and thought to murder him when Jacob officially received the birthright blessing (see Genesis 27:26–41). But, my, how gracious Esau grew to be, as evidenced when his and Jacob's caravans met in the desert many years later!

> And the messengers returned to Jacob, saying, We came to thy brother Esau, and also he cometh to meet thee, and four hundred men with him.
>
> Then Jacob was greatly afraid and distressed: and he divided the people that was with him, and the flocks, and herds, and the camels, into two bands. (Genesis 32:6–7.)

As a present for Esau, Jacob sent on ahead several hundred of his domestic animals. Finally the two brothers met.

> And [Esau] said, What meanest thou by all this drove which I met? And he said, These are to find grace in the sight of my lord.
>
> And Esau said, I have enough, my brother; keep that thou hast unto thyself.
>
> And Jacob said, Nay, I pray thee, if now I have found grace in thy sight, then receive my present at my hand: for therefore I have seen thy face, as though I had seen the face of God, and thou was pleased with me. (Genesis 33:8–10.)

Where are those synagogues now in which it was once so desperately important for some to maintain their place rather than to confess publicly their belief in Jesus? (See John 12:42–43.) Later, some of those who hesitated may have acquired the necessary courage.

> And the word of God increased; and the number of the disciples multiplied in Jerusalem greatly; and a great company of the priests were obedient to the faith (Acts 6:7).

The list of such bracing and reminding questions could be multiplied almost indefinitely.

If, over the decades, one could have been agelessly situated on a space platform and could have thus watched the recurring human drama from a distance, among the strongest impressions he would have acquired would be the dull repetitiveness of human folly. He would see the almost childish intensity with which each new set of players on this planet pursues the cares of the world.

The age-old drama goes on, with each group pursuing the cares of the world as if they were pioneers in the process instead of constituting just another legion of lemmings marching to the secular sea.

How does the adversary get away with it? Mostly by darkening the human mind. Who, after all, would purchase his wares in the bright light of day, when their shoddiness and pale imitativeness could be more clearly seen—to say nothing of the appalling consumer consequences flowing from use of his wares?

Among other things, the adversary also induces new jargon to describe old sins. He also provides new rationalizations to justify old vices. Mostly, however, he can count on new crops of greenies!

The adversary cleverly uses the tight time frame of mortality against morality to undercut the purposes of mortality. Thus he is able in a variety of ways to persuade many mortals to believe of this life, "This is it! This is all there is!" "Go for the praise and honor of men, because that is all there is!" "Seek sensations while they last, to verify that you are really alive."

By cleverly steering people away from the reality of immortality and accountability, he uses endless variations in the same, basic, recurring theme: "Eat, drink, and be merry, for tomorrow we die" (2 Nephi 28:7, 8).

Hence each new generation not only acts out the drama but does so with a prideful provincialism— as if there were nothing to be learned from the past. Moreover, if the permissive generation still prefers to believe at all in a God, they will believe in a permissive God.

The human appetites are thus pandered to— whether it be the desire for ascendancy, for pornography, for alcohol, or for drugs. Physical beauty is admired regardless of the lack of spiritual beauty in some such individuals. High cheek bones are desirable even if accompanied by low morals. "Conspicuous consumption" is fashionable, whether in things material or things sensual.

Indeed, though we may not comprehend this next reality fully, the adversary understands it well: "The spirit indeed is willing but the flesh is weak" (Matthew 26:41). He understands, far better than we, that when temptations come to us mortals, there actually is at least one way to escape or to bear:

> There hath no temptation taken you but such as is
> common to man: but God is faithful, who will not
> suffer you to be tempted above that ye are able; but
> will with the temptation also make a way to escape,
> that ye may be able to bear it (1 Corinthians 10:13).

Unsurprisingly, the adversary neither encourages us to search for the ways to escape nor to outlast the challenge.

The more inaccessible or unused mankind's moral memory is—that is, the holy scriptures—the more provincial mortals become, and hence the more intense their participation in the recurring drama in which the cares of the world usually triumph.

Besides, are not the cares of the world so easy to care about?

The very repetitiveness of the cares of the world can thus make their claim on us predominant. Such cares can also create a self-serving rhythm to life, be it humdrum hedonism, humdrum humanism, or hum-drum nihilism.

Once we are desensitized and dulled by the cares of the world, the routine of schedules and merely sur-viving becomes so consuming, so self-reinforcing, and so self-serving. Though we might be stirred to resist an outright political dictatorship, the dominating cares of the world keep us compliantly in our places. Thus, scarcely sensing what might have been, we are con-tented with what is.

So each generation is consumed with building sand castles which the tides of time soon wash away, clear-ing the beach just in time for the next "tourists" to start the whole process anew.

For the faithful, however, who see "things as they really are and . . . things as they really will be" (Jacob 4:13), there is a precious perspective in knowing which are the things of most worth, which are the "weightier matters" (Matthew 23:23). Similarly, it can be very helpful to know why this world was created (see Isaiah 45:18) and why we are here. When we truly know how caring of us God is, then we know what to care about.

Our Gracious and Merciful God
(Nehemiah 9:17)

It is one of the ironies of religious history that many mortals err in their understanding of the nature of God and end up rejecting not the real God but their own erroneous and stereotypical image of God. Frequently this is because they have thought of God solely in terms of thunderings at Sinai without pondering substance:

> And the Lord descended in the cloud, and stood with him there, and proclaimed the name of the Lord.
> And the Lord passed by before him, and proclaimed, The Lord, The Lord God, merciful and gracious, longsuffering, and abundant in goodness and truth. (Exodus 34:5–6.)

At several points in the scriptures God is described as using a voice which was neither loud nor harsh.

Third Nephi 11:3 is an example. Elsewhere we read of God's being gracious, merciful, and of great kindness:

> . . . neither were [they] mindful of thy wonders that thou didst among them; but hardened their necks, and in their rebellion appointed a captain to return to their bondage; but thou art a God ready to pardon, gracious and merciful, slow to anger, and of great kindness, and forsookest them not (Nehemiah 9:17).

Since we are to strive to become like the Father and the Son (see Matthew 5:48, 3 Nephi 12:48; 27:27), the adjectives which describe them are vital for us to note carefully and then to strive to emulate diligently. Therefore, all we can learn of God, His nature, and His attributes is essential to our faith and spiritual progress.

There is utility as well as beauty in developing each of these qualities:

> The merciful man doeth good to his own soul: but he that is cruel troubleth his own flesh (Proverbs 11:17).

This further insight underlines another of the happy consequences of developing the cardinal virtues:

> By mercy and truth iniquity is purged: and by the fear of the Lord men depart from evil (Proverbs 16:6).

Mercy can purge the soul of sin, making room for a fresh start. Truth is vital in order that we have an unvarying standard by which to determine what we are to be and to do and what we are to rid ourselves of.

All the cardinal virtues, therefore, carry their own intrinsic as well as outward reward. A merciful man *does* do good to his own soul.

It is interesting to compare certain thoughts our Savior declared, first as Jehovah and later as Jesus:

> He hath shewed thee, O man, what is good; and what doth the Lord require of thee, but to do justly, and to love mercy, and to walk humbly with thy God? (Micah 6:8.)

> Wo unto you, scribes and Pharisees, hypocrites! for ye pay tithe of mint and anise and cummin, and have omitted the weightier matters of the law, judgment, mercy, and faith: these ought ye to have done, and not to leave the other undone (Matthew 23:23).

We are even warned by the Apostle James about exercising judgment without mercy.

> For he shall have judgment without mercy, that hath shewed no mercy; and mercy rejoiceth against judgment (James 2:13).

Surely we worship a God who is perfectly just and merciful, and these perfected attributes are reflected in His plans for us:

> And now the plan of mercy could not be brought about except an atonement should be made; therefore God himself atoneth for the sins of the world, to bring about the plan of mercy, to appease the demands of justice, that God might be a perfect, just God, and a merciful God also (Alma 42:15).

Our God does not indulge us, but He is merciful toward our weaknesses as He strives to tutor us:

> But now I tell it unto you, and ye are blessed, not because of your iniquity, neither your hearts of unbelief; for verily some of you are guilty before me, but I will be merciful unto your weakness (D&C 38:14).

Our God is not careless, either, with regard to His divine standards. But given our human imperfections, His plan, by its very nature, has to be a plan of mercy or it could not redeem (see Alma 42:15).

Therefore, as we strive to become as the Father is and as Jesus is, we are to become more gracious and merciful, more kind and considerate. Even more, we are to do this in a world which does little to encourage such qualities of character.

In this harsh and darwinistic world there are even those who argue that there is danger of one's being taken in or used if he or she is too gracious and merciful. This concept sparks the creation of "clever" catchphrases such as, "If the meek are going to inherit the earth, they must become more aggressive." But disciples would rather trust at the risk of being mistaken occasionally than live suspiciously or mistrustfully.

C. S. Lewis pointed out that some people are angry with God for His not existing, and others for His existing but for failing to do as mortals would have Him do. Instead of such childishness, we are urged to know God and to learn of His attributes.

In the *Lectures on Faith,* a course taught in the Kirtland period in the school of the prophets, one of the stipulated essentials to having real and true faith is to have a correct understanding of the character, personality, and perfections of God. Without such an understanding, people can become very confused. By misunderstanding the nature of God they will also misunderstand the purpose of life and of themselves as well.

Some mistakenly misread the mercy and graciousness of God. For instance, some partial believers are always scolding God, or disregarding Him, because of the observable and lamentable consequences of our misuse of God's gift to us of moral agency. It is as if a teenage son, given his first car, promptly had an accident with resulting pain, suffering, and expense, and the errant son then railed at his father for permitting the suffering resulting from the son's misuse of the gift of the automobile.

Granted, in defense of the analogy, mortal parents ought not to give youngsters automobiles too soon, and then only when they have provided wise counsel, driver training, and so on. But there still comes a time when, if they are ever to drive alone, trained teenagers must be left alone at the wheel. The principle is the same with us in the second estate.

It is one of the great ironies of human history that some mortals with incorrect understanding of God and life's purposes sometimes scold God because of the abundance of human misery and suffering—which, indeed, lies all about us. Such individuals almost dare God to demonstrate His existence by straightening things out—and at once!

But He is a much different kind of Father than that. Surely it is requisite to eternal life that we come to know God and Jesus Christ whom He has sent (see John 17:3).

The Father's meekness is seen in the timbre of His voice . . . not harsh and loud but small and piercing (see 3 Nephi 11:3). To come to know God and His will and voice is a vital achievement. Otherwise we can, instead, so easily be led by the adversary "at his will" because we have failed to hearken to the voice of God (see Moses 4:4).

This meekness is also seen in His gracious deference to His Son. Through a process of divine investiture, most of the words of our Heavenly Father have come to us through His only Begotten Son, Jesus Christ. Because there are only a few special circumstances in which we have the Father's words, certainly and directly, these are especially worthy of our pondering.

Among these rare moments are the words of the

Father given at Jesus' baptism; on the Mount of Transfiguration; at Jerusalem; upon introducing the resurrected Jesus in the Americas; and, similarly, in
Palmyra's Sacred Grove. Respectively, here are the
scriptures recording those occasions:

> And lo a voice from heaven, saying, This is my
> beloved Son, in whom I am well pleased (Matthew
> 3:17).

> While he yet spake, behold, a bright cloud over-
> shadowed them: and behold a voice out of the
> cloud, which said, This is my beloved Son, in whom
> I am well pleased; hear ye him (Matthew 17:5).

> Father, glorify thy name. Then came there a voice
> from heaven, saying, I have both glorified it, and
> will glorify it again. (John 12:28.)

(Jesus said of this last instance [verse 30] that the
audibility was "for your sakes," that the people who
were proximate might know.)

> Behold my Beloved Son, in whom I am well
> pleased, in whom I have glorified my name—hear
> ye him (3 Nephi 11:7).

> This is My Beloved Son. Hear Him! (Joseph Smith—
> History 1:17.)

Divine investiture is defined as that condition in
which

> in all His dealings with the human family Jesus the
> Son has represented and yet represents Elohim His
> Father in power and authority. . . . Thus . . . Jesus
> Christ spoke and ministered and through the
> Father's name; and so far as power, authority, and
> Godship are concerned His words and acts were
> and are those of the Father. (James E. Talmage,
> *Articles of Faith,* pp. 470–71.)

There is, however, yet another remarkable episode in the Book of Mormon recorded for us by Nephi, who foresaw the baptism of Jesus centuries *before* it occurred:

> And the Father said: Repent ye, repent ye, and be baptized in the name of my Beloved Son (2 Nephi 31:11).

Further Fatherly endorsement was reported by Nephi a few verses later:

> And I heard a voice from the Father, saying: Yea, the words of my Beloved are true and faithful. He that endureth to the end, the same shall be saved. (2 Nephi 31:15.)

How rare! How precious! How endorsing of Jesus! How instructive to us as to the importance of enduring to the end!

It is striking that these rare words of endorsement and deference, directly from the Father, underscore certain things. *First,* they *testify* of His approval of His Redeeming Son and of the Father's relationship to His Only Begotten. *Second,* they *urge* us mortals to follow His Son by repenting and being baptized in the name of His Son. *Third,* they *certify* that Jesus' words are true. *Fourth,* they *exhort* us to endure to the end.

Perhaps what these verses from the Book of Mormon thus give us is a more complete account of what the Father said at the baptism of Jesus than we have in the New Testament Gospels.

> And lo a voice from heaven, saying, This is my beloved Son, in whom I am well pleased (Matthew 3:17; see also Mark 1:11, Luke 3:22).

Or these words of the Father may have been heard and reported only by Nephi. Either way, the words of

the Father are not only sparingly given but are
strikingly simple. These Fatherly affirmations and
exhortations cannot be safely ignored.

In the special setting in which the Father's words
were heard, Nephi also heard the words of the Son:

> And also, the voice of the Son came unto me,
> saying: He that is baptized in my name, to him will
> the Father give the Holy Ghost, like unto me;
> wherefore, follow me, and do the things which ye
> have seen me do (2 Nephi 31:12).

A Father, perfect not only in His power but also in
His kindness and graciousness, so strikingly defers to
His Son! It was this Son of whom certain villagers
remarked on "the gracious words which proceeded
out of his mouth" (Luke 4:22).

Graciousness, kindness, and mercifulness. How
worthy of emulation and how crucial of acquisition!

Nor should we overlook how summationally the
gospel can be expressed:

> Now this is the commandment: Repent, all ye ends
> of the earth, and come unto me and be baptized in
> my name, that ye may be sanctified by the reception
> of the Holy Ghost, that ye may stand spotless before
> me at the last day.
>
> Verily, verily, I say unto you, this is my gospel;
> and ye know the things that ye must do in my
> church; for the works which ye have seen me do
> that shall ye also do; for that which ye have seen me
> do even that shall ye do. (3 Nephi 27:20–21.)

When one comes to know God and His Son Jesus
Christ through the scriptures, the Spirit, and personal
revelation, it is impossible to feel anything other than
overwhelmed by the attributes so perfectly developed
in them and so tentatively and superficially developed
in oneself. Even so, we are told to strive to become like
them.

Moses, we read, was "very meek, above all the men which were upon the face of the earth" (Numbers 12:3). Yet on at least one occasion he was not meek enough and did not follow the Lord's instructions. When the people of ancient Israel and their animals needed water, Moses was told to speak to the rock and bring forth water, but instead he struck the rock twice with his rod. In rashness, Moses said, "must we fetch you water," calling the people, "Ye rebels" (Numbers 20:7–12). This is noted concerning the remarkable and special man Moses simply to make the point that Jesus is the only person who has lived upon this planet who was perfect in His meekness. Yet a merciful God still tutored and readied Moses for later duties, such as the stunning episode on the Mount of Transfiguration.

Peter learned, too, about the Lord's reaction to rashness when he cut off the right ear of the high priest's servant; Jesus promptly reproved him for this and then restored the ear (see John 18:10; Luke 22:50–51). Oh, how gracious and merciful is our God throughout all generations!

On the Mount, together, were Moses and Peter, and how much that tells us!

This is the Lord Jesus who chose Galilean fishermen; the Jehovah who chose a lad with a slingshot to face Goliath; the God who chose Enoch, who was slow of speech and hated by all the people. This pattern should convey to all of us a humbling sense of security, for our God is a God of love. He waits with open arms, and the unfolding of His merciful plan of salvation is not only therefore the mark of divine power but also the mark of God's relentless, redeeming love.

It is a point well worth pondering because, among other reasons, it will help us to understand better why God, through the prophets, denounces sin and corrup-

tion in such scalding terms. He loves all of us, His spirit
sons and daughters, but hates our vices. His denun-
ciation of those vices may, if we are not careful, seem
to obscure the enormous and perfect love He has for
us. John Donne put it well:

> I do not love a man, except I hate his vices, because
> those vices are the enemies, and the destruction of
> that friend whom I love (*Donne's Prebend Sermons,*
> p. 177).

On a divine and perfect scale, that is how God
regards our sins, but how also He regards us.

There is also the very real possibility that, in the
justice of God, one of the reasons He uses the weak and
the foolish of the world is so that no argument could
be made later that certain people were advantaged in
some unfair way by that which was unearned —either
in the premortal life or here. Hence it seems prudent
for us to realize that just because one is set apart or
ordained to a certain calling or assignment he or she
must not expect to be set apart from the stresses of life.
There appear to be no immunities.

There are some obvious reasons for this. All of us
must walk the same strait and narrow path, know the
same kind of experiences as those we would seek to
lead and to serve. There is not one strait and narrow
path for the officers—the chosen—and another for the
enlisted men. We are all to experience life "according
to the flesh"; there is no other way, for it is the way to
immortality and eternal life. Given the resplendent
riches of the promised kingdom, why would anyone
wish to walk another path than the one that leads us
back to our gracious and merciful Father in Heaven?

"Distress of Nations, With Perplexity"

(Luke 21:25)

It is clear to all thoughtful souls that life on this planet is precariously perched as never before—except for the days of Noah and the deluge.

Given our twentieth-century level of development, this might appear paradoxical. Mankind has access to unparalleled technology. Average lifespans have lengthened considerably. Communication is at an unprecedented peak. Crop yields can be dramatically increased.

Ours has all the potential for a golden age, yet instead it is an age of burgeoning anxiety and unsettlement. Thousands starve. An arms race threatens global terror. Drug traffic increases and even intertwines with governments. Pornography spreads as a multi-billion dollar business. Key problems elude solutions, and such solutions as are reached result frequently in merely fixing things which do not stay fixed. Indeed, a prophecy of the Savior is being filled even as we watch: the nations of the world are experiencing "the distress of nations, with perplexity" (Luke 21:25).

There are several other scriptures which speak of some unusual, specific, and composite conditions preceding the second coming of the Savior.

> And in that day shall be heard of wars and rumors of wars, and the whole earth shall be in commotion, and men's hearts shall fail them, and they shall say that Christ delayeth his coming until the end of the earth (D&C 45:26).

> And all things shall be in commotion; and surely, men's hearts shall fail them; for fear shall come upon all people (D&C 88:91).

> But when ye shall hear of wars and commotions, be not terrified: for these things must first come to pass; but the end is not by and by (Luke 21:9).

> Men's hearts failing them for fear, and for looking after those things which are coming on the earth: for the powers of heaven shall be shaken (Luke 21:26).

A response to these verses might cause one to miss the fact that the "whole earth shall be in commotion," contributing undoubtedly to a condition in which "men's hearts shall fail them" and in which fear "shall come upon all people."

Some of that fear will exist because of "those things which are coming." Much of this "commotion" may be geophysical, with earthquakes, seas heaving themselves beyond their bounds, and other cataclysmic events.

> For after your testimony cometh the testimony of earthquakes, that shall cause groanings in the midst of her, and men shall fall upon the ground and shall not be able to stand (D&C 88:89).

But the basic unsettlement of "all things" may reflect the seismology of a sensual, secular society. The sense of being unanchored will be pervasive and will pertain to "all things," including the shifting relationships among nations, the overturning of traditional moral values, and the widespread political instability. All such events will finally center in the feelings inside individuals. The wars and multi-caused commotions will produce "distress of nations, with perplexity."

"Perplexity" refers to a confused mental state concerning the conditions of things, a sense of bewilderment. "Commotion" can be defined as a circumstance, individual or collective, of unrest, uncertainty, and upheaval.

Thus, while much of this confused condition will understandably and justifiably be attributable to wars and rumors of wars, to fear and anxiety over conflicts on the planet, it would be superficial to look only at those obvious causes without exploring and noting the underlying conditions which brought about those symptoms. The unsettled, unspiritual state of much of mankind, the confusion over moral values, the uncertainty over the purpose of life and the reality of Deity—these will all contribute mightily.

Though the ultimate and collective expressions of the world's malaise spring partly from political and military symptoms, the sense of commotion may therefore be rooted in spiritual causes rather than exclusively and solely in geophysical and political ones. This demonstrates how easy it is for galloping fear to turn into fatalism, bewilderment, or abandonment.

These circumstances will include that foreseen by Peter, in which, among other things, "truth shall be evil spoken of" (2 Peter 2:2).

No wonder the Lord, through Isaiah, spoke in special reproof of those who create upheaval in traditional and correct values.

> Woe unto them that call evil good, and good evil; that put darkness for light, and light for darkness; that put bitter for sweet, and sweet for bitter! (Isaiah 5:20; see also 2 Nephi 15:20.)

Once the light of Christ, which has been given to every man (D&C 84:46) is dimmed, if not extinguished, then the capacity people have to know good from evil is largely gone, and this creates ultimate confusion and ultimate darkness.

> For behold, my brethren, it is given unto you to judge, that ye may know good from evil; and the way to judge is as plain, that ye may know with a perfect knowledge, as the daylight is from the dark night.
>
> For behold, the Spirit of Christ is given to every man, that he may know good from evil; wherefore, I show unto you the way to judge; for every thing which inviteth to do good, and to persuade to believe in Christ, is sent forth by the power and gift of Christ; wherefore ye may know with a perfect knowledge it is of God.
>
> But whatsoever thing persuadeth men to do evil, and believe not in Christ, and deny him, and serve not God, then ye may know with a perfect knowledge it is of the devil; for after this manner doth the devil work, for he persuadeth no man to do good, no, not one; neither do his angels; neither do they who subject themselves unto him. (Moroni 7:15–17.)

Significantly, verse 17 notes that neither the devil nor his angels persuade people to do that which is good, and "neither do they who subject themselves unto him." Those who subject themselves to the adversary and do his work, about whom Isaiah spoke, have their modern counterparts who will condemn for evil that in which there is not evil (see D&C 64:16). Likewise with those who lift up their heel against the Lord's anointed to cry that the Lord's anointed have sinned, when they have not sinned (see D&C 121:16).

The malaise stems in large measure from a widespread disbelieving in God or from relegating Him to a minor role in the universe, causing an upheaval in the realm of traditional and true values.

All of this and much more creates the unrest and uncertainty and upheaval. The resultant commotion causes men's hearts to fail them. Hence the fear and anxiety and bewilderment within man—to say nothing of the external disorders in the natural world which will precede the second coming of the Son of Man.

Indeed, if wars are made in the hearts and minds of men, how much more disorder, how much more war and conflict, are made in the hearts and minds of *despiritualized* men and women in an environment in which "all things shall be in commotion"!

Given the commotions noted above, it will be likely that, for instance, in international relations things will not hold still.

In a time of "perplexity of nations," it will be difficult for nations (whether regarding their political or economic systems) to resolve anything and have it stay resolved. Even if accords are reached that aim at achieving long-term security—political, economic, or military—such will likely prove elusive of sustained implementation . . . "till there [is] no remedy" (2 Chronicles 36:16).

Thus, when systems cannot be counted upon to deliver, such is merely the collective and outward manifestation of *individuals* who can no longer be counted upon, because they themselves are confused.

Let us focus briefly, not comprehensively, on one vexing problem to illustrate the prophesied commotion, perplexity, and complexity. Merely outlining that complexity can be illustrative.

The prospect or at least the possibility of nuclear war overhangs us and our time. It is a unique condition and a challenge which has men and women almost vying for attention as they describe the awesome threat. The threat is surely real enough. Wars may be actually fought with nuclear weapons in the future. The overriding concern, though exploited by some for their own ancillary purposes, is clearly justified as possibilities such as an ensuing "nuclear winter" press upon us.

The whole matter presents a panorama of intriguing questions with which altogether too few have genuinely wrestled.

For instance, should governments, long ago, have acted in enforceable concert by insisting that their scientists be less free, thereby retarding if not preventing the discovery of atomic energy and the splitting of the atom? There are few who, upon reflection, would have had the world's scientists be less free. Moreover, such global, intergovernmental cooperation, for one reason or another, was not obtainable in the 1930s, 1940s, and 1950s. Whether a deep and shared desire exists now to try to achieve such cooperation will, before long, be seen. Can there be an interval of peace based upon the mutual interests in arms reduction? Millions sincerely hope so.

Should there have been established for the sake of humanity the equivalent of a Pax Britannica, a single political state, to which all other nations would have ceded their sovereignty and which would have thereby an enforceable monopoly on nuclear weapons?

There are not many of us mortals who would trust such a monopoly, regardless of any such benefits, including a Pax Americana. It was Churchill with his eloquence who marked a time of limited possession of nuclear weapons, when there were only two such national powers, but these "two atomic collossi [were] malevolently eyeing each other over a trembling world." "Malevolently eyeing" each other now are numerous nations possessing or soon to reach the capacity to make nuclear war. Besides, nationalism is on the rise.

The prickly questions continue:

Should some among the human family quickly and sincerely promote unilateral pacifism? Even if it appears unlikely to become universal?

In any event, would this be a pacifism without an accompanying righteousness? The contagious pacifism of which we read in the scriptures describes those who would not make war, even in self-defense, but instead trusted in the blessings of God (see Alma 24:17–27). Can we recommend unconditional pacifism or uni-lateral disarmament for any people who are not other-wise righteous and therefore are unable to rely on the Lord to bless them? Would the citizens of Sodom have been spared if they had been pacifists but otherwise unrighteous? Or does unilateral disarmament constitute undue reliance upon the arm of flesh and natural man?

Should we go on solely exhorting and blaming in-cumbent political leaders in nation after nation who fail to achieve disarmament, even if, comparatively, the internal pressures placed upon them to do so are grossly uneven?

It is a very complex challenge. If the will for peace is universal and deep, why then do so many political

leaders get away with violating that will? The need to
"renounce war and proclaim peace" (D&C 98:16) is so
obviously simple.

Are we not, therefore, now seeing a prophecy fulfilled—not only with regard to war, but also as to other
challenges, such as international debt—when, on the
earth, there will be "distress of nations, with perplexity"?* (Luke 21:25; see also D&C 88:79.)
Perplexity is defined as "complicated, confused,
troubled and bewildered."

But surely, it is sincerely asserted, nations must see
that they must try and must trust. They must at least
make a start. To fail is absurd. The need to negotiate is
so obvious. Self-interest alone makes clear the path to
be pursued.

It is precisely at this point that something ominous
becomes more clear: the terrible price we are paying
for secularized man.

If man's brotherhood is biological only, temporary
only; if the Fatherhood of God is no longer an oper-
ating moral imperative; if past and present treaties and
international organizations have proven inadequate to
the task; if this life is all there is—out of what reservoir
of hope, goodness, and trust do we expect to draw suf-
ficient, universal goodwill to underwrite such sorely
needed negotiations?

Desperation is not inspiration. The requirements to
be shared by all nations in order to achieve such peace
are nothing short of breathtaking.

But, it will be quickly said, cannot those with
religious faith cooperate fully with agnostics and
atheists for common survival?

---

*Other translations of this verse include: "anguish of nations, not
knowing the way out. . . ." (New World Translation); "The nations will
be in dismay, bewildered. . . ." (Moffatt)

It would seem so. Then why is it not all happening? Do we really believe that a half-dozen leaders can frustrate a concern and a hope so deeply and universally held? It includes but is much more than "a communication problem."

Moreover, is it intellectually honest for some to extract and to invoke certain anticipatory and prophetic language from the scriptures, such as that from the Old Testament about beating our "swords into plowshares" and "spears into pruninghooks" (Isaiah 2:4), *without* noting how that condition is to be achieved? For it will happen with the coming of the Messiah. These promises rest on specific premises. They will occur in a setting in which the Messiah, Jesus Christ, will usher in a millennial reign during which there will be worldwide peace.

Furthermore, if the United Nations diagnosis of 1945 is correct and war begins in the hearts and minds of men, how hopeful for the future can we be if more and more families are failing and if our educational systems are too often bereft of moral content? These two are mainstay institutions which profoundly shape the hearts and minds of men.

Poverty and conspiracy combine to create more terrorists each year than we can produce peacemakers in a generation. In this regard, we have yet to plumb the depths of these verses with all their implications as to greed and envy:

> But it is not given that one man should possess that which is above another, wherefore the world lieth in sin (D&C 49:20).

> Neither shalt thou desire . . . any thing that is thy neighbour's (Deuteronomy 5:21).

With so many variables at work, can there be true concern over nuclear war, and over education concerning the dangers of nuclear war, if this concern is treated apart from all the other conditions incident to peace? Even if the major powers, for instance, achieve concord concerning nuclear weapons, will this prevent terrorists from bringing nuclear holocaust upon mankind anyway? Or the use of other, non-nuclear means of destruction, such as chemical or germ warfare, which may prove even more resistant to international accord and real control?

In other words, can the challenges attendant to avoiding nuclear war really be dealt with apart from the need for general righteousness on this planet?

If failure tragically results (see Zechariah 14:2; Malachi 4:1; 2 Nephi 27:2; 2 Nephi 6:15), will the various political systems bear the full guilt? Or will individuals? Or will both? (See JST Matthew 24:31.)

If, for instance, a person samples the Ten Commandments, he will be forced to conclude that we can scarcely expect genuine and widespread peace to prevail if people engage in stealing—whether land or goods. How much security can there be if people tell lies and bear false witness against each other? If people are guilty of covetousness, or if people engage in murder, there can be no real peace.

Today, those aggrieved can act out their vengeance in many ways and on an awesome scale. The urge for revenge, for instance, is as real as ever, only now what was once the adjoining village is all mankind!

Can there, in fact, be peace in the world if there is not peace in our homes as well as in our hearts? Can we, in fact, really expect to have peace in the world if the civil wars raging inside so many individuals do not subside? Or, if there is rampant and desensitizing sexual immorality, adultery, and all things "like unto it" tearing at the fabric of individual souls and families? Or, just when we especially need mortal minds at their best in order to deal with complexity, if enslaving and desensitizing drugs are more and more pervasive?

The vices of humanity are far more interactive than many people realize. In the societies of Sodom and Gomorrah there was rampant sexual immorality; there was also inordinate pride, idleness, and a neglect of the poor and the needy. (Ezekiel 16:48–50.) A haughty attitude towards God (who had given strict counsel on the need to care for the poor) led to the neglect of the poor and the needy. This is something those who would focus all of their attention on poverty, without any concern for adultery and homosexuality—and vice versa—would do well to ponder upon.

But some will quickly say that the requirements of generalized righteousness are too exacting and too unmanageable for mankind and, therefore, if we rely upon this ultimate solution, then nuclear war is inevitable. Something else, they say, must be done, even if the solution is secular. It is hoped for by many that treaties, for instance, may be negotiated which will rest upon shared fear; treaties which are verifiable, even if nations do not care for or trust each other.

Christians are often chided, sometimes rightly, because some of us do not do as we have been told to do: "renounce war and proclaim peace" (D&C 98:16). We would do well to look to our own posture with regard to peace and our responsibilities to be peacemakers.

At the same time, perhaps we cannot be fully blamed if we are not reflexively enthusiastic about the approach to peace which many would use, when it is so bereft of accompanying general spiritual content. Yes, there was repentant Nineveh. Yes, there have been intervals of peace in human history. But time and space have collapsed, and man's interdependence has never been as pronounced as now.

But what of man's dependence on God?

Surely, as Latter-day Saints we must avoid the Jonah reflex. Moreover, knowing of and believing in the prophecies does not relieve us of the responsibility to do all we can to avoid the conditons which, un- checked, will bring them to pass.

Jesus also prophesied that in the last days, because of iniquity, the love of many would wax cold (Matthew 24:12). Yet we must not regard iniquity or human hardening and coarsening with a sense of inevitability.

"Wise as serpents, and harmless as doves"? (Matthew 10:16.) Without wisdom and with too few genuine doves, there will be a mounting "distress of nations, with perplexity."

By the way, *harmless* denotes "without guile"— that is, without duplicity, trickiness, deceitful cunning, and so on. To be guileless is to be innocent of such traits—even at the risk of appearing naive. (See Alma 18:22; D&C 111:11.)

Significantly, "to be without sin"—or innocent— is what is being conveyed, not an endorsement of niaveté. It will be to and through those of integrity and innocence that the Lord's help can best be given in seeking to solve one of the most complex of human problems, the global expression of which cannot be fully addressed without also addressing the individual and personal requirements of peace.

James summed it up well:

> From whence come wars and fightings among you? come they not hence, even of your lusts that war in your members?
>
> Ye lust, and have not: ye kill, and desire to have, and cannot obtain: ye fight and war, yet ye have not, because ye ask not. (James 4:1–2.)

Thus true peace is tied to human righteousness— irrevocably. Moreover, Church members are genuinely helping the cause of peace as we follow Jesus' injunction to "seek not the things of this world but seek ye first to build up the kingdom of God, and *to establish his righteousness"* (JST Matthew 6:38; italics added; see also KJV Matthew 6:33).

In a time of "distress of nations, with perplexity" Church members can help contribute significantly in other ways as well. For instance, an LDS scientist might help with the technology of deterrence, detection, or verification in a way which would advance the cause of negotiated peace. Others might assist in the relief of disease, famine, or other destabilizing conditions.

But what comes "first" is clear: The gospel seed fully flourishes only in certain soil, the same soil in which true peace can grow.

"Not Without Honour, Save in His Own Country, and in His Own House"

(Matthew 13:57)

In studying and pondering the early ministry and life of Jesus, as we learn more about His divine nature we learn much too about human nature. For instance, there was the inability or unwillingness of many to receive saving truths from Someone who was in their midst. Because they had known that person, He seemed in some respects ordinary instead of ordained. Even though Jesus said and did objectively impressive things, which ought to have given an objective onlooker pause, the tendency to disregard or denigrate Him was strong: "Oh yes, I know all about him!"

The tendency to rely on too small a sample and to use the lazy shorthand way of assessing prophets is present today, as if driving repeatedly through a university campus were knowing a university. But that which is familiar is not necessarily always understood.

When He was but twelve, young Jesus astonished those with whom He discussed the scriptures in the temple at Jerusalem.

> And it came to pass, that after three days they found him in the temple, sitting in the midst of the doctors, both hearing them, and asking them questions.
> And all that heard him were astonished at his understanding and answers. (Luke 2:46–47.)

There was also the later time when He went—with what expectations or nostalgia we know not—back to "his own country," to Galilee's Nazareth and Capernaum. His neighbors heard Him read and comment upon the scriptures:

> And all bare him witness, and wondered at the gracious words which proceeded out of his mouth.
> And they said, Is not this Joseph's son? (Luke 4:22.)

They were truly impressed. Yet they asked, "Is not this Joseph's son?"

Mark's writings, too, indicate how impressed His own people were as Jesus spoke to them in their own country. They marveled at His wisdom and His works. No doubt they had heard of His miracles. (Mark 6:1–6.) Matthew says they were astonished at His "wisdom and these mighty works" (Matthew 13:53–58).

Yet all of this was discounted or dismissed by some because in their view, after all, "Jesus was Joseph the carpenter's son."

In His sermon in one synagogue, Jesus boldly declared His Lordship. He was rejected, and some of the people even tried to throw Him off the brow of a hill. And this after His miraculous feeding of the five thousand, word of which cannot have escaped the attention of those present.

Jesus' preachment in Capernaum was rejected because the son of Joseph, the carpenter, declared Himself to be the bread of life, sent down from heaven. (See John 6:35, 38.)

Out of these episodes of rejection came Jesus' lamentation that "a prophet is not without honour, save in his own country, and in his own house." (Matthew 13:57.)

Familiarity got in the way of their recognizing Jesus' divinity.

Instead of truly assessing Him, they used labels— "the carpenter's son"—to classify Him. Past proximity caused townsfolk and kinsmen alike to regard Him with indifference.

In addition to the problems caused by familiarity and proximity, something else was present. Though subtle, this insight must not escape us. There was apparently no objection to Jesus' Sermon on the Mount. However, the Sermon at Capernaum caused a violent reaction. Why? Because in the sermon at Capernaum, Jesus declared His Lordship! The more declarative He was, the more restive His audience and the more attrition among His followers. The more specific His message, the more difficult He was to follow, hence:

> From that time many of his disciples went back, and walked no more with him (John 6:66).

There was a clear lack not only of intellectual objectivity but also of ordinary curiosity which might have led some to assess and to evaluate Jesus instead of dismissing Him in such a peremptory way.

Though Jesus was perfect and Joseph Smith was not, the same pattern is seen in responses to the latter's message and mission. Had Joseph not brought forth additional scriptures but instead contented himself with being another itinerant, charismatic preacher, stirred by a preceding spiritual experience, the reaction of the world to him would have been otherwise too.

But it was Joseph's declarativeness, under the tutoring of the resurrected Jesus, which unsettled so many. Hence the rush, even today, to seek demeaning or easy explanations for Joseph Smith, such as those to be found in his environment or in the activities of his father and family. Some will do anything to avoid paying attention to the astonishing truths Joseph taught.

Back, however, to Galilee. Living in Nazareth and Capernaum were some of Jesus' relatives and kinsman. How did these individuals respond? They said, "Go away":

> His brethren therefore said unto him, Depart hence,
> and go into Judaea, that thy disciples also may see
> the works that thou doest (John 7:3).

Why? "For neither did his brethren believe in him" (John 7:5). To a degree not known fully to us, Jesus was, alas, "without honour in his own house."

Ironically, this was the only instance in human history when townsmen had a chance to keep the first and second commandments simultaneously: to love a Neighbor and a God at the same time!

Shortly after these episodes in His own country, Jesus went to Jerusalem's Feast of the Tabernacles. Once again, He was vastly impressive.

> And the Jews marvelled, saying, How knoweth this
> man letters, having never learned? (John 7:15.)

In spite of being so impressed, however, as soon as Jesus waxed declarative about whose doctrine He preached—God's—their reactions changed. Furthermore, as He reproved the people for not keeping the law of Moses, He was accused of being a devil and of being paranoid: "Who goeth about to kill thee?" (John 7:20).

There was as much provincialism in urbane Jerusalem as in Capernaum.

It all forms a pattern, the significance of which must not be lost upon us. Human nature has not changed, including the ways in which many people respond to prophets. Insularity often leads to indifference, even insolence. Thus Jesus encountered not only erroneous expectations about the Messiah, but intellectual laziness as well.

Why does this happen? Because, living daily among us, a prophet is seen as being merely one of us. How, therefore, can he be more than us?

The perversity of human nature is busily at work too, as in the familiar imagery of lobsters trying unsuccessfully to crawl out of a barrel; no lobster is allowed to ascend to the top, because his neighbors soon reach up and pull him back down. Not only misery but commonality too likes company.

In the calling of David seven of Jesse's sons had passed in review, but the unsatisfied seer asked if these were all.

> The Lord said unto Samuel, Look not on his countenance, or on the height of his stature; because I have refused him: for the Lord seeth not as man seeth; for man looketh on the outward appearance, but the Lord looketh on the heart (1 Samuel 16:7).

Then, almost as an afterthought, David, the youngest, was mentioned. But he was out keeping the sheep. Surely it wouldn't be he who would be called!

Paul, in his epistles, indicated at least one reaction to his outward appearance and to his personality. Some people regarded his letters as powerful and weighty, but his bodily presence as weak (see 2 Corinthians 10:10). His speech was regarded as rude, or contemptible (see 2 Corinthians 11:6).

In the Revised Standard Version of the New Testament, 2 Corinthians 10:10 is rendered thusly: "For they say, His letters are weighty and strong, but his bodily presence is weak, and his speech of no account."

Paul is portrayed as saying, "Even if I am unskilled in speaking, I am not in knowledge; in every way we have made this plain to you in all things." (2 Corinthians 11:6, Revised Standard Version.)

Moffatt renders 2 Corinthians 10:10 as follows: "My opponent says, Paul's letters are weighty in telling, but his personality is weak and his delivery was beneath contempt." In 2 Corinthians 11:6 in that version Paul declares, "I am no speaker, perhaps, but knowledge I do possess; I have never failed to make myself intelligible to you."

Thus the absence of a commanding physical presence—or, in modern political terms, the absence of charisma—can cause people to disregard or dismiss one actually sent of God, even though the substance of the individual or his message is exceedingly important.

A pseudo-sophisticated society is especially likely to dismiss someone who does not have impeccable educational credentials. Impressive as Peter and John were, they were still labeled:

> Now when they saw the boldness of Peter and John, and perceived that they were unlearned and ignorant men, they marvelled; and they took knowledge of them, that they had been with Jesus (Acts 4:13).

As always, the adversary manages to have it both ways. Educated and articulate Paul, learned by worldly standards, gave a great discourse before King Agrippa, yet Agrippa turned Paul's learning against that prophet by saying, "Much learning doth make thee mad" (Acts 26:24).

Prophets can be dismissed or discounted in many ways. If their faults can be focused upon, their message can be dismissed. Or, if they can be labeled, they need not be listened to (winebibber, Sabbath breaker, unlearned, ignorant, and so forth). Or, if they can be denigrated in some other way, their message can be discounted.

It is humbling to observe what prophets themselves have said about their faults. Moroni, for example:

> And if there be faults they be the faults of a man. But behold, we know no fault; nevertheless God knoweth all things (Mormon 8:17).

> Condemn me not because of mine imperfection, neither my father, because of his imperfection, neither them who have written before him; but rather give thanks unto God that he hath made manifest unto you our imperfections, that ye may learn to be more wise than we have been (Mormon 9:31).

Since the Church is for the perfecting of the Saints, obviously we will experience each others' faults; and we are to understand this and to help influence others in doing likewise:

> Turn to the Lord with all your mind, might, and strength; that ye lead away the hearts of no more to do wickedly; but rather return unto them, and acknowledge your faults and that wrong which ye have done (Alma 39:13).

> Brethren, if a man be overtaken in a fault, ye which are spiritual, restore such an one in the spirit of meekness; considering thyself, lest thou also be tempted (Galatians 6:1).

Surely among the "burdens" we bear are each other's failings in a second estate in which the process of spiritual growth involves so much proving, re-proving, and thereby improving.

> Any member of the church of Christ transgressing, or being overtaken in a fault, shall be dealt with as the scriptures direct (D&C 20:80).

> Admonish him in his faults, and also receive ad-monition of him. Be patient; be sober; be temperate; have patience, faith, hope and charity. (D&C 6:19.)

> Cease to be idle; cease to be unclean; cease to find fault one with another (D&C 88:124).

Additionally, even more rigorous requirements are laid upon us:

> For what glory is it, if, when ye be buffeted for your faults, ye shall take it patiently? but if, when ye do well, and suffer for it, ye take it patiently, this is acceptable with God (1 Peter 2:20).

> And it came to pass that he said unto them: Behold, here are the waters of Mormon (for thus were they called) and now, as ye are desirous to come into the fold of God, and to be called his people, and are willing to bear one another's burdens, that they be light;
>   Yea, and are willing to mourn with those that mourn; yea, and comfort those that stand in need of comfort, and to stand as witnesses of God at all times and in all things, and in all places that ye may be in, even until death, that ye may be redeemed of God, and be numbered with those of the first resur-rection, that ye may have eternal life. (Mosiah 18:8–9.)

Not only are each others' faults clearly among the burdens we bear. We are even given help in terms of how we are to manage certain circumstances in which we feel each other's faults and see each other's short-comings:

> Moreover if thy brother shall trespass against thee, go and tell him his fault between thee and him alone: if he shall hear thee, thou hast gained thy brother (Matthew 18:15).

> Confess your faults one to another, and pray one for another, that ye may be healed. The effectual fervent prayer of a righteous man availeth much. (James 5:16.)

The prophets were, and are, human enough to feel rejection, especially from family. Nevertheless the aforecited lamentation over the failure to accord the prophet the honor due him is not simply to plead for sympathy concerning a prophet's feelings of rejection. On the contrary, the real concern is that the hearers fail to receive the message. Prophets want to be heard for the latter reason; they are only marginally concerned about the acceptance of themselves. After all, they can carry on in the midst of rejection—as did Ether, from the rising of the sun to its setting—even when their success is minimal (see Ether 12:3).

In modern times Joseph Smith's mission, then and now, proves to be no exception to Jesus' utterance about the lack of familial honour accorded prophets (see Matthew 13:57). He was blessed by steady Hyrum but vexed by well-meaning but mercurial William.

The Prophet Joseph, on April 7, 1844, on a Sunday afternoon occupying the Nauvoo temple stand, said, "We are looked upon by God as though we were in eternity." The Prophet noted that we must remember that God dwells in eternity and that He does not see things as we do (see *The Words of Joseph Smith*, p. 346). This perspective, no doubt, aided Joseph in coping with what was heaped upon him.

This great and restoring prophet, just a month before his martyrdom, also observed that "God will always protect me until my mission is fulfilled" (p. 367), because Joseph was involved in laying "a foundation that will revolutionize the whole world" (p. 367).

Interesting, isn't it, that he would use that word *revolutionize?* The Prophet's grandfather, Asael Smith, observed years before that one of his posterity would, in fact, "revolutionize" the world of religious thought. Three separate memories of Asael's words follow:

> My grandfather, Asael Smith, long ago predicted that there would be a prophet raised up in his family, and my grandmother was fully satisfied that it was fulfilled in me. My grandfather Asael died in East Stockholm, St. Lawrence county, New York, after having received the Book of Mormon, and read it nearly through; and he declared that I was the very Prophet that he had long known would come in his family. (Joseph Smith, *History of the Church,* 2:443.)

> My grandfather, Asael Smith, heard of the coming forth of the Book of Mormon, and he said it was true, for he knew that something would turn up in his family that would revolutionize the world (George A. Smith, *Journal of Discourses* 5:102).

> Among the snow-clad hills which rise above the Canadian boundary, in the state of New York, is today a lone and simple grave of a meek and humble man. The winds and the storms of eighty-six winters have defaced the mound, and the ravages of time have beaten bare the tombstone which once bore his name. But there, under the sod and dew, rest the mortal remains of an aged patriarch who, in the course of his life, made the wonderful prediction that out of his posterity would arise one who would be sent of God to bring joy and peace to the souls of

men; whose mission would be to bring new light and truth into a night of darkness; and who would revolutionize the world of religious thought. (Joseph Smith Fish, "A Grandfather's Prediction" [*Improvement Era,* January 1917], p. 207.)

"It has been borne in upon my soul that one of my descendants will promulgate a work to revolutionize the world of religious faith." (Asael Smith, quoted in E. Cecil McGavin, *The Family of Joseph Smith* [Bookcraft, 1963], p. 1.)

For instance, even the ancestors of Joseph Smith were prepared beforehand.

It was decreed in the counsels of eternity, long before the foundations of the earth were laid, that he, Joseph Smith, should be the man, in the last dispensation of this world, to bring forth the word of God to the people, and receive the fulness of the keys and power of the Priesthood of the Son of God. The Lord had his eyes upon him, and upon his father, and upon his father's father, and upon their progenitors clear back to Abraham, and from Abraham to the flood, from the flood to Enoch, and from Enoch to Adam. He has watched that family and that blood as it has circulated from its fountain to the birth of that man. He was foreordained in eternity to preside over this last dispensation. (John A. Widtsoe, comp., *Discourses of Brigham Young* [Deseret Book Company, 1946], p. 108.)

As an example of this, there was the brave Reverend Lathrop. Born at Etton, England, and christened in the little church there, Lathrop later broke with the there dominant church because of its lack of apostolic authority. He established one of the first Congregational churches in the London area, for which he was put in jail. His wife and children suffered in his absence, and finally his wife died. Released from prison, Reverend Lathrop brought his family and flock to America and settled in the Barnstable, Massachusetts, area.

Lathrop was Joseph Smith's fifth great-grandfather, one of the preeminent ancestors to whom Brigham Young referred.

Our perfect God prepares the lineage of His prophets beforehand and honors them in their ministries. Meanwhile, imperfect mortals usually pass them by and notice them not, let alone honor them.

The failure to search the scriptures with intellectual meekness is one cause of the failure to notice.

Jesus' having grown up in Nazareth apparently confused Jewish scholars. Because the Messiah was to be born in Bethlehem and because of lost scripture, they evidently assumed that He would be reared there also (see Matthew 2:23; John 7:42). So it is that among the many questions put to Jesus in His mortal ministry, there is no record of anyone's having asked Jesus where He was born! The obscurity factor again.

As to the historicity of Jesus and other great spiritual leaders, critics would do well to not overreact to the seeming silence of the secular record.

There are, after all, those imponderables which proceed from imperfect and inadequate information. There is the general silence of the secular record that proceeds from the discounting of things spiritual. There is also the comparative silence which proceeds from the press of the cares of the day, because of which spiritual things are little, if at all, noticed. Incomplete data, therefore, yield incomplete conclusions. Silence is not automatic refutation.

Caution is particularly appropriate for yet another reason. Even in modern history, such as the events surrounding the December 1941 Japanese attack on Pearl Harbor (where there are an abundance of data and still living witnesses), there are now conflicting conclusions and conflicting views about the degree to which American leaders were aware that such an attack was coming. If there can be conflicting conclusions concerning things so recent, in the face of abundant data, how much more careful we should be regarding conclusions in a setting of sparse data and of antiquity!

Moreover, some treat the pieces of information which comprise history as if they were the fragments in a kaleidoscope—with the facts rearranging themselves at the mere shake of the next viewer. Hence, we get revisions of revisions of revisions.

This is not to say that the effort to create authentic and accurate history should not be undertaken. Rather, it is to say that caution and intellectual meekness should be the order of the day. Meanwhile, Sir Winston Churchill's caution about the limitation of history is worth heeding: "History with its flickering lamp stumbles along the trail of the past, trying to reconstruct its scenes, to revive its echoes, and kindle with pale gleams the passion of former days" (*Churchill Speaks: Collected Speeches in Peace and War,* Robert Rhodes James, ed. [Windward, 1981], p. 734).

Meanwhile, wise historians will be the first to forgive those nonhistorians who, while interested, prefer to be patient until the perfect day. Then all will be known, and we will see, but not through glass darkly!

Finally, prophets, like all of us, are accountable to God. He is their final judge, not we.

So often, when there is a rush to judgment, there is a rash judgment—a most unwise circumstance in view of the fact that all of us will one day kneel and our tongues will confess that Jesus is the Christ. Further-

more, we will likewise acknowledge openly that all
God's judgments are just!

> But this cannot be; we must come forth and *stand*
> *before him* in his glory, and in his power, and in his
> might, majesty, and dominion, *and acknowledge* to
> our everlasting shame *that all his judgments are*
> *just*; that he is just in all his works, *and that he is*
> *merciful* unto the children of men, and that he has
> all power to save every man that believeth on his
> name and bringeth forth fruit meet for repentance
> (Alma 12:15; italics added).

In view of this reality we should be more concerned with how we, individually, will fare at that
critical moment. We will then be supplicants, not
wearers of the robes of a judge—least of all to judge
the prophets of God! Meanwhile, if we and ours would
be blessed, let us honor God's prophets in our families
and neighborhoods and countries. The lessons of
history are clear as to the esteem due the Lord's
anointed.

SERMON NUMBER SIX

"*Wicked and Adulterous Generation*"
(Matthew 16:4)

All serious readers of the scriptures are familiar with the instances in which Jesus juxtaposed particular adjectives, which was more than accidental.

Then certain of the scribes and of the Pharisees answered, saying, Master, we would see a sign from thee.

But he answered and said unto them, An *evil* and *adulterous* generation seeketh after a sign; and there shall no sign be given to it, but the sign of the prophet Jonas. (Matthew 12:38–39; italics added.)

A *wicked* and *adulterous* generation seeketh after a sign; and there shall no sign be given unto it, but the sign of the prophet Jonas. And he left them, and departed. (Matthew 16:4; italics added.)

Whosoever therefore shall be ashamed of me and of my words in this adulterous and sinful generation; of him also shall the Son of man be ashamed, when he cometh in the glory of his Father with the holy angels (Mark 8:38).

Why that particular juxtaposition? Why not "wicked and merciless generation"? Or "wicked and proud generation"? Such words might have been equally and descriptively accurate. But the linkage with sexual immorality is too deliberate to ignore.

Sexual sin leads to a loss of faith, and sometimes to a craving for signs, as this episode recounted by the Prophet Joseph illustrates.

> When I was preaching in Philadelphia, a Quaker called out for a sign. I told him to be still. After the sermon, he again asked for a sign. I told the congregation the man was an adulterer; that a wicked and adulterous generation seeketh after a sign; and that the Lord had said to me in a revelation, that any man who wanted a sign was an adulterous person. "It is true," cried one, "for I caught him in the very act," which the man afterwards confessed when he was baptized. (*Teachings of the Prophet Joseph Smith*, pp. 277–78.)

As is so often the case, there are multiple levels of meaning in the inspired words of scripture. Moreover, Jesus' scalding generalization clearly fits more than the generation to whom it was originally given.

First, a few illustrative episodes concerning the quest for signs and demonstrative miracles.

> And the Lord spake unto Moses and unto Aaron, saying,
>
> When Pharaoh shall speak unto you, saying, Shew a miracle for you: then thou shalt say unto Aaron, Take thy rod, and cast it before Pharaoh, and it shall become a serpent.
>
> And Moses and Aaron went in unto Pharaoh, and they did so as the Lord had commanded: and

> Aaron cast down his rod before Pharaoh, and before
> his servants, and it became a serpent.
>
> Then Pharaoh also called the wise men and the
> sorcerers: now the magicians of Egypt, they also did
> in like manner with their enchantments.
>
> For they cast down every man his rod, and they
> became serpents: but Aaron's rod swallowed up
> their rods. (Exodus 7:8–12.)

In spite of the above extraordinary events, so far as
the record indicates there were no "converts" in
Pharaoh's court. Divine power was demonstrated and
opportunities for the softening of hearts were there,
but there were no lasting spiritual gains.

Nor is the craving for signs confined to pagan unbelievers.

> Then answered the Jews and said unto him, What
> sign shewest thou unto us, seeing that thou doest
> these things? (John 2:18.)

> Then said Jesus unto him, Except ye see signs and
> wonders, ye will not believe (John 4:48).

But true faith cannot be developed by or depend
upon a perpetual "Star Wars" of signs and wonders.
Yet the quests and demands for such have been in evi-
dence throughout all time:

> And it came to pass that he said unto me: Show me a
> sign by this power of the Holy Ghost, in the which
> ye know so much (Jacob 7:13).

> And now Korihor said unto Alma: If thou wilt show
> me a sign, that I may be convinced that there is a
> God, yea, show unto me that he hath power, and
> then will I be convinced of the truth of thy words
> (Alma 30:43).

> Yea, there are many who do say: If thou wilt show
> unto us a sign from heaven, then we shall know of a
> surety; then we shall believe (Alma 32:17).

Usually, even when a sign is given to an unbeliever, any ensuing appreciation or humility does not last, because such people are too dependent upon compulsion or intimidation. (See also Alma 32:13.)

Besides, true subjects do not dictate terms to their King.

> And others, tempting him, sought of him a sign from heaven (Luke 11:16).

Nor is it merely the unlettered who so quest; curiosity reaches the highest levels, as it did with adulterous Herod (see Mark 6:17, 18):

> And when Herod saw Jesus, he was exceeding glad: for he was desirous to see him of a long season, because he had heard many things of him; and he hoped to have seen some miracle done by him (Luke 23:8).

Sign-seeking shaped responses to Christ and His message not only during His mortal ministry but long after His crucifixion and atonement:

> For the Jews require a sign, and the Greeks seek after wisdom (1 Corinthians 1:22).

So signs there may be, but for unbelievers such usually produce no spiritual betterment.

> And he that seeketh signs shall see signs, but not unto salvation (D&C 63:7).

It cannot be otherwise if mortality is to be a true test of faith:

> And now, I, Moroni, would speak somewhat concerning these things; I would show unto the world that faith is things which are hoped for and not seen . . . for ye receive no witness until after the trial of your faith (Ether 12:6).

It is much the same with the principle of hope:

For we are saved by hope: but hope that is seen is
not hope: for what a man seeth, why doth he yet
hope for?
     But if we hope for that we see not, then do we
with patience wait for it. (Romans 8:24–25.)

In the foregoing context, the significance of the
juxtaposition of those particular adjectives, *wicked* and
adulterous, may now be further examined.

First of all, the people of the world cannot presume
to command God to provide them with signs. A person
can neither be a disciple and command the Master nor
can he require "perpetual renewal of absolute proof."
Some behave, however, as if they would set forth the
conditions under which they will believe—complete
with specifications; they then invite God to "bid" on
their specifications!

Furthermore, as noted, the constant provision of
validating signs would violate the intrinsic and vital
role of faith in the second estate (see Ether 12:6). President Brigham Young said, "There is no saving faith
merely upon acknowledging a fact" (*Journal of Discourses,* 7:55).

Sign seekers, like adulterers, often do have a clear
preference for *repeated* sensation. Those who do not
understand why adultery is intrinsically wrong will
also fail to understand why faith is a justified requirement laid upon us by God. We are to walk by faith and
to overcome by faith (see D&C 76:53).

Those who will not humble themselves "because
of the word" (see Alma 32:14–16) are no different than
the magicians of Pharaoh's court. Those men must
have been impressed by the miracles which came from
the Lord through Moses. But their proximate reactions
made no ultimate difference! The magicians merely be-

came hardened again, as if to say, "What has the Lord shown us lately?"

By contrast, the faithful, who are intellectually honest but are confronted with new and present challenges, sing of the Lord, "We've proved Him in days that are past."

How long would the Sanhedrin have remained interested in Jesus Christ even if He had appeared to them after His resurrection? Or Pilate? The remarkable visions enjoyed by Sidney Rigdon were not, in fact, able to keep him humble "because of the word." A little time away from the Saints was enough to reignite his vanity.

But to continue the analysis:

Those who are adulterous have also a strong preference for "now" rather than for eternity. Impatience and incontinence, quite naturally, team up.

Such erring individuals or generations also have a strong preference for meeting the needs of "me" over attending to others, a lifestyle which speeds selfishness on its endless, empty journey.

By making demands of God, the proud would attach conditions to their discipleship. But discipleship requires of us unconditional surrender to the Lord. Hence the proud neither understand nor really love God. Therefore they violate the first commandment by seeing God as a sign provider upon request; as a function, not a tutoring Father.

Is this not precisely how some regard their sexual partners, as something to be used and then dismissed or discarded?

But God will not be used:

> Ye ask, and receive not, because ye ask amiss, that
> ye may consume it upon your lusts (James 4:3).

Yet God is ever ready to respond when a request is right.

Ask not, that ye may consume it on your lusts, but ask with a firmness unshaken, that ye will yield to no temptation, but that ye will serve the true and living God (Mormon 9:28; see also 3 Nephi 18:20).

Nor does God, who is perfect in mercy, require perfection of us before He responds. If we are seeking and striving, it is a beginning which is welcomed and rewarded with gifts:

For verily I say unto you, they are given for the benefit of those who love me and keep all my commandments, *and him that seeketh so to do;* that all may be benefited that seek or that ask of me, that ask and not for a sign that they may consume it upon their lusts (D&C 46:9; italics added).

Clearly, in examining Jesus' words *wicked and adulterous generation* we are dealing, therefore, not only with the true nature of faith but with the true nature of real love as well—whether love of God or of man.

Henry Fairlie, in his excellent book *The Seven Deadly Sins Today,* contrasts lust and love:

Lust is not interested in its partners, but only in the gratification of its own craving, not in the satisfaction of our whole natures, but only in the appeasement of an appetite that we are unable to subdue. . . . Lust dies at the next dawn, and when it returns in the evening, to search where it may, it is with its own past erased. . . .

Some of the evils to which theology says that Lust will give rise are: blindness of intellect in respect of divine things; precipitancy in acting without judgment; want of regard for what befits one's state or person; inconstancy in good; hatred of God as an Avenger of such sins; love of this world and its pleasures; inordinate fear of death. Even if we set aside those that are directly concerned with our relationship with God, we are still left with the fact that Lust, no less than the other sins, affects our conduct and attitudes to life in ways beyond its own immediate interests. . . .

The lustful person will usually be found to have a terrible hollowness at the center of his life, and he is agitated to fill it, not daring to desist, lest he should have to confront the desert he has made of himself and his life. He has no spiritual resource to which to turn. (Henry Fairlie, *The Seven Deadly Sins Today* [Washington, D.C.: New Republic Books, 1978], pp. 175, 185, 187.)

Thus we see that the first commandment and the seventh commandment are intrinsically tied together . . . as are wickedness and adulterous interactive.

Sensual individuals are users, not builders; they are takers, not givers; demanders, not producers. They are carnal, not spiritual. They are often the victims of self-deception, as was Korihor. His self-deception reached such enormous proportions because it was "pleasing unto the carnal mind" (Alma 30:53).

From this analysis a caution emerges for Church members today: as wickedness and adultery (*and things like unto it*) increase in the world, there will be made of disciples even more strident demands for signs. Likewise, because iniquity is increasing in the world, the love of many will wax cold (see Matthew 24:12; D&C 45:27). (Not only more demands, but less mercy and compassion.)

Therefore, in a sensual, secular society, we should expect more mocking when proof is not supplied upon demand.

Disciples will be restrained as always, however, from urging the giving of such signs, because these come only from the Lord and on the conditions He determines (see D&C 24:13). Hence there will inevitably be more criticism and more cynicism as people seek, and even demand, signs, but "not unto salvation."

As in the days of Noah, people will also be preoccupied with the cares and the pleasures of the world (see Matthew 24:37). Ironically, most therefore will even miss such signs as God gives pertaining to Jesus' glorious second coming. Instead, the desensitized and unnoticing in self-dissuasion will say (just as prophesied in the scriptures), "All things continue as they were from the beginning of the creation" (2 Peter 3:3–4). Humdrum hedonism camouflages much critical data. By diminishing our capacity to feel, it also diminishes our capacity to serve others. Despair robs us of hope, and immorality of faith and love. What, then, of faith, hope, and charity?

There is an increasing test especially intriguing in a desensitized, secular society which can be applied to almost any circumstance in order to demonstrate the importance of our knowing about the gospel's plan of salvation. If one can really be persuaded that he is not only watched over by the Lord but is also compassed about by a great cloud of past witnesses and preceding kinsmen, will he not behave differently? In this sense it is really ludicrous, therefore, to speak in terms of a private morality, or even of a private moment. This is hard doctrine, however, in a society of sign seekers.

The notion that private immorality is somehow acceptable rests on the notion that certain behavior is "safe" because it is confined. Just as there can be no private smallpox or cholera, at least one other individual is usually affected by our sin, and usually more, whether immediately or eventually.

Likewise the diminished self whom the immoral person becomes deprives his associates of the privilege of associating with one who is more whole and serene and helpful. Since sin is a war against our very nature, we err if we think that this war can be safely confined.

Civil wars have a way of spreading ever so subtly and are the most vicious of all wars.

The false notion of private morality is inflated in our time because celebrated sinners often get so much sanctioning attention by the media. Ignored is their representation of raw selfishness and raw appetite. In fact, such people are sometimes touted as being bold, even brave, and as worthy of envy. Yet their "good time" does not last even in this life, for illness and loneliness finally claim their own. Even the enemies of the Church who receive the "praise of the world" often find that "they themselves shall be despised by those that flattered them" (D&C 121:20).

The truth is, however, that their conduct is often so grossly wrong as to be anything but praiseworthy. Would we applaud someone who is being consumed by maggots? Or award a marksmen medal to someone who has just shot himself in his foot? Our compassion should be given to those thus self-distressed and self-conflicted. But our praise? Never!

Chances are very good that if a person can accept this reality of being watched over, he or she will behave differently. We really are, even when we seem to be alone, part of a loving heavenly family who would have us behave so as to be happy.

Once persuaded that life is a continuum, and likewise that one will never cease to exist, and further that the wrongs we do must be painfully undone and any missteps retraced—once so persuaded, how careful we then are concerning what we do and what we think and what we become!

This macro and spiritual view is, of course, in stark contrast to those who urge, "Eat, drink, and be merry," because "you only live once!" The gospel response to that assertion is "Yes, we only live once, but that once is forever!" How constant the contest between the spiritual and the sensual, and how different the consequences, as Jesus' prophecy foretold.

As the foregoing attempts to illustrate, divine deliberateness was at work when the Lord juxtaposed two words so directly as He has done with "wicked and adulterous generation." There is a wealth of meaning and relevancy to be derived from the scriptures, if we are serious students of them.

Yes, searching the scriptures is labor, but it can come to be a labor of love and a journey of discovery.

"Search the Scriptures"
(John 5:39)

Among the things we Latter-day Saints need to do is to increase our sophistication in the use of the scriptures.

John Donne speaks about "dilating" the scriptures, enlarging them so that we might see their true spiritual scope and significance.

The prophetic, God-given power to declare doctrine was given to the Prophet Joseph Smith. Otherwise, what John Donne said is true: "The best men are Problematicall, Onely the Holy Ghost is Dogmaticall" (*Donne's Prebend Sermons,* p. 12). So we had best study carefully the doctrines revealed through prophets as contained in holy writ.

For instance, we should recognize that certain scriptures commingle prophecies which bear upon different time periods. The classic example is chapter 24 of Matthew, in which Jesus prophesying both about events which were to happen soon and events then quite distant.

The destruction of the temple (see Matthew 24:1–12) occurred within a few decades, but the foreseen calamities preceding the Second Coming (see, for instance, Matthew 24:21, 22) were still centuries away.

The same time duality is found in section 87 of the Doctrine and Covenants (see D&C 87:1–6). The section contains revelation given on Christmas Day, 1832, and deals most directly with the prophecy that the rebellion and the resultant Civil War in the United States would begin at South Carolina, even though the firing on Fort Sumter was then about three decades away.

Significantly, that prophesy warns of "the death and misery of many souls." The Civil War was, indeed, a bloody war, resulting in about 204,000 battle casualties plus another 225,000 military personnel who died of disease. This number actually well exceeds the American battle deaths (128,000) in World War I. In World War II, there were 396,637 battle deaths.

In one two-day Civil War battle alone, Chickamauga, 35,000 were killed or wounded out of 128,000 soldiers. The Americans killed in the Viet Nam war, a war which stretched over ten years and which jarred American life profoundly in many ways, totaled around 60,000.

Section 87 also speaks of "wars" (verse 1), suggesting not one war but a continuum of conflict. Thus, like chapter 24 of Matthew, this scripture covered things both imminent and distant.

Furthermore, verse 4 speaks of a time . . . "after many days" . . . when slaves would rise against their masters. True, some slaves fought in the Civil War, but these words may suggest something of far greater portent.

So too with verse 5, which speaks about "the remnants" on the land, the seed of Jacob who will rise up to "vex the Gentiles"; an intriguing and sobering prophecy, obviously involving developments far beyond the events of the American Civil War.

As to the "wars" being a continuum (see verse 1), World War I was terribly bloody, costing 7½ million battle casualties (dead, wounded, missing, etc.), plus millions of civilian deaths from flu and other diseases. Books have been written to show the profound impact of World War I on Western civilization—an impact far beyond battle casualties.

> The idea of endless war as an inevitable condition of modern life would seem to have become seriously available to the imagination around 1916. Events, never far behindhand in fleshing out the nightmares of imagination, obliged with the Spanish War, the Second World War, the Greek War, the Korean War, the Arab-Israeli War, and the Vietnam War. It was not long after the second World War, says Alfred Kazin, that even most liberal intellectuals abandoned the hope that that war had really put an end to something. (Paul Fussell, *The Great War and Modern Memory* [New York: Oxford University Press, 1975], p. 74.)

Another wrote, ". . . War is the continued experience of the Twentieth century man."

Of course, in our own time, we could add the war in Afghanistan, Iran and Iraq, civil wars in Central America, Lebanon, the British-Argentine conflict, etc. These are sobering comments, especially when placed in this scriptural context:

> For I am no respecter of persons, and will that all men shall know that the day speedily cometh; the hour is not yet, but is nigh at hand, when peace shall

be taken from the earth, and the devil shall have
power over his own dominion (D&C 1:35).

And in that day shall be heard of wars and rumors of
wars, and the whole earth shall be in commotion,
and men's hearts shall fail them, and they shall say
that Christ delayeth his coming until the end of the
earth (D&C 45:26).

Given the reported tragedy of unnecessary war,
one might even wonder aloud as in Cowper's lines:

"But war's a game, which, were their subjects wise,
    Kings would not play at."
                          ("The Winter Morning Walk").

As we search the scriptures, it should be part of our
sophistication too to be able to see relationships between scriptural truths and the human condition.

One scripture, for example, portrays people in the
latter days as wandering or running to and fro in search
of the truth and not finding it (see Amos 8:11–12).
Such words do not, however, describe all of mankind,
by any means.*

As in centuries past, therefore, many mortals are
disinterested in real religion, because they have been
enveloped in irreligious secularism or have been disap-
pointed or desolated by false religion. Many have
simply become too busy in the work of the world.

In Isaiah's remarkable prophesy contained in the
first part of chapter 24 of his book, we read that the
"haughty people of the earth do languish" (Isaiah
24:5). One rendering of the words "haughty people" is
the "upper class." *Languish* connotes a drooping, a

---

*To use another example, the Lord's "army," or Church, will become
"very great" (see D&C 105:31) compared to its present size, and though
the Saints will be "scattered upon all the face of the earth." Nevertheless,
comparatively, its numbers will be "few" and its dominions "small" (see
1 Nephi 14:12–14).

spiritlessness, a loss of animation. Significantly, Nephi also used the word *droop* in addressing his soul—"No longer droop in sin." (2 Nephi 4:28.)

Granted, the seekers add up to "many" (D&C 123:12). But most mortals are preoccupied with the cares and anxieties of the world.

In the above context one thinks, for instance, of the upper class such as was portrayed in the Public Broadcasting System's *Brideshead Revisited.* At least some of the upper class of England were, in fact, a spent people. For them, life had lost its meaning; even their frivolity showed their boredom and their sense of emptiness.

Just how, over decades of time, the upper classes —the opinion molders, the influence makers—have interacted with and affected others in various societies would require the analysis of a gifted psychologist-historian. However, these reflections of Aleksandr Solzhenitsyn about the "first whiff of secularism" in his native land and about the growing disbelief of the upper class in earlier Russia are one illustration:

> Different parts of the world have followed different paths, but today they are all approaching the threshold of a common ruin.
>
> In its past, Russia did know a time when the social ideal was not fame, or riches, or material success, but a pious way of life. . . . Faith was the shaping and unifying force of the nation. But in the seventeenth century . . . Russia felt the first whiff of secularism; its subtle poisons permeated the educated classes in the course of the nineteenth century. . . . By the time of the Revolution, faith had virtually disappeared in Russian educated circles; among the uneducated, too, faith had declined. (Aleksandr Solzhenitsyn, "Men Have Forgotten God," *National Review,* July 22, 1983, p. 374.)

Secularism, the setting in which most Christians will live out their lives, is both a diversion from and a perversion of life's true purpose. Hence the disappointment in the secular search for the meaning of life. Hence the drooping of the human spirit in which the conscience can come to be regarded as an intruder. Indeed, ennui, boredom, and humdrum hedonism are descriptive of those thus afflicted, as this lamentation indicates:

> Are all men's lives . . . broken, tumultuous, agonized and unromantic, punctuated by screams, imbecilities, agonies and death? Who knows? . . . I don't know. . . . Why can't people have what they want? The things were all there to content everybody, yet everybody got the wrong thing. I don't know. It's beyond me. It's all darkness. (Public Broadcasting System production of "The Good Soldier," presented in early 1983.)

Thus, while we usually think of apostasy solely in terms of theological deviation, we often fail to see its connections to the everyday, human condition in which the consequences of that deviation are enormous.

To continue the suggestion about connecting up the scriptures and the human condition, the words of Isaiah indicate that the dwellers of the earth will be "desolate" (Isaiah 24:6). "Desolate" connotes joylessness or a grief-stricken condition—a state kindred to the spiritlessness which the word *languish* connotes.

Why did all this happen? Because, said Isaiah, the people had "transgressed the laws, changed the ordinances, broken the everlasting covenant" (Isaiah 24:5). When such basic breakdowns happen, then sweeping and sad consequences follow.

We see still other symptoms in our own time. As prophesied by the Savior, "because iniquity shall abound, the love of many shall wax cold" (Matthew 24:12). The capacity of human beings to love— whether it is love of God, of life, or of others—shrinks in a climate of iniquity.

As life thus loses its meaning and purpose for those so afflicted, despair replaces joy. Anomie or drift drive out purpose. When people mock God's messengers and despise His words, deterioration sets in "till there [is] no remedy" (see 2 Chronicles 36:16).

No remedy but One!

The remedy, the redemption, of course, is to be found in Jesus and His encompassing and emancipating message. He is the centerpiece of human history, the validation and verification of the meaning of life. He is the Executor of Our Father's glorious and redemptive "plan of happiness" (Alma 42:8). And it is He about whom the scriptures testify so abundantly:

> Search the scriptures; for in them ye think ye have eternal life: and they are they which testify of me (John 5:39).

Peter foresaw that heresies and apostasies would have at their center the ultimate deviation: to denigrate and to "deny the Lord that bought them" (2 Peter 2:1). For those so mistaken, the denial of Jesus and of His purchasing atonement dissolves the meaning and purpose of life. With this denial, for those so deluded, any assurance of immortality and individuality and personal accountability exit also (see 1 Corinthians 6:20). Men are then left to try to find their own ways:

> In those days there was no king in Israel, but every man did that which was right in his own eyes (Judges 17:6; see also Judges 21:25).

> They seek not the Lord to establish his righteousness, but every man walketh in his own way, and after the image of his own god, whose image is

in the likeness of the world, and whose substance is
that of an idol, which waxeth old and shall perish in
Babylon, even Babylon the great, which shall fall
(D&C 1:16).

What we often fail to add, however, in our declar-
ations about the Restoration, is the glorious perspective which the restoration and the full gospel give to us
about the meaning of life on this planet and the unfold-
ingness of God's plan of salvation. It is this, too, which
can give meaning to life and which can remedy those
conditions in which people languish and droop and are
desolate. An aristocracy of Saints is what is needed,
since finally no other aristocracy can really lead the
way—certainly not any like the "haughty people"
Isaiah saw.

In a great many ways we are therefore bearers of a
message of far greater and deeper significance than we
can now possibly imagine.

The restored gospel is thus a gospel of hope and
meaning: not a vague, generalized hope but a message
of specific and justified hope for which myriad mortals hunger and which all mortals need.

One major example is the verification of the reality
of the resurrection. This came initially with the theo-
phany of the First Vision. Later, too, with the visita-
tions of other resurrected beings. Also with the witness
of additional scriptures.

Verification of the resurrection came too in still
other ways, such as modern visions. On Sunday
morning, April 16, 1843, on the temple stand at
Nauvoo, the Prophet Joseph spoke. As recorded by
Willard Richards, Joseph spoke of a vision (about
which, alas, we apparently do not have any other information) concerning "those who have died in Jesus
Christ." The vision was so plain that "I actually saw
men, before they ascended from the tomb, as though

they were getting up slowly, they took each other by the hand and it was my father and my son, my mother and my daughter, my brother and my sister" (*The Words of Joseph Smith,* p. 195). Quite humanly, the Prophet indicated "more painful to me the thought of annihilation than death."

It is that very sense of impending annihilation and nothingness which bothers a great many mortals today and enshrouds their lives in despair. The Prophet also noted how "the expectation of seeing my friends in the morning of the resurrection cheers my soul," and helped him to "bear up against the evils of life" (p. 196).

The Prophet rejoiced in the clarity of this vision and sought to prepare his people for the storms which were ready "to burst upon you like peals of thunder" but "all your losses will be made up to you in the resurrection provided you continue faithful" (p. 196). He then declared, "By the vision of the Almighty, I have seen it."

Joseph then further affirmed that "God has revealed His Son from the heavens. And the doctrine of the resurrection also."

No wonder the Prophet further observed, "It is my meditation all day and more than my meat and drink to know how I shall make the saints of God to comprehend the visions that roll like an overflowing surge, before my mind" (p. 196).

The Prophet reflected and then exclaimed, Alma-like, "Hosanna. Hosanna. Hosanna, to Almighty God that rays of light begin to burst forth upon us even now. . . . O that I had the language of the archangel to express my feeling. . . ." (P. 196; see also Alma 29:1.)

The "good news" of the Restoration is for those marvelous mortals of all races, creeds, and cultures who already believe in God and His purposes but who can now have added reason to believe.

It is for those who partially believe but who need convincing cause to become true believers.

It is for those especially noted herein for whom life seems empty and who are filled with despair but who do still, in fact, wander or run to and fro in search of the truth . . . but do not know where to find it.

How vital the restoration of modern revelation— both institutional and personal! For as the Prophet also observed, "Could you gaze in heaven five minutes you would know more than you possibly can know by reading all that ever was written on the subject" (*The Words of Joseph Smith,* p. 254).

Thus the holy scriptures are relevance themselves if we will but search and apply them "for our profit and learning" (1 Nephi 19:23).

In further demonstration of the *verity, beauty,* and *diversity* of the scriptures, a comparison of the Ten Commandments as set forth in the twentieth chapter of Exodus and the fifth chapter of Deuteronomy and in the tenth chapter of Mark is interesting (see Mark 10:17–22). For the rich, righteous young man, Jesus apparently did not mention the requirement of avoiding profanity and keeping the Sabbath day holy. For what reason we know not. Perhaps comment was not required. The Savior did substitute "defraud not" for the requirement of avoiding covetousness. But he omitted the Sabbath day and profanity, as he did the commandment concerning idolatry. Whether those mentioned were what Jesus wished to stress to that young man or to the particular audience, we simply do not know. Certainly Jesus was no less interested in the keeping of the Sabbath day and the other commandments he did not mention on this occasion.

This incident suggests how, with propriety, spiritual emphasis may be given one time which differs from a previous or a later emphasis. Such, for instance, was the case in Joseph Smith's recitations of the First Vision, with differing emphases appropriate to differing audiences.

Not only are there intriguing truths only partially disclosed in holy scriptures, in terms of their implications, but there are also some individuals about whom we would especially desire to know more and about whom one day we shall. Gamaliel the Pharisee was such an individual; he was a much-respected doctor of the law (see Acts 5:34). Paul had been one of his pupils (see Acts 22:3). Gamaliel used his influence on one occasion in the Sanhedrin to give appropriate counsel which benefited the work of the Lord.

> Then stood there up one in the council, a Pharisee, named Gamaliel, a doctor of the law, had in reputation among all the people, and commanded to put the apostles forth a little space;
>
> And said unto them, Ye men of Israel, take heed to yourselves what ye intend to do as touching these men.
>
> For before these days rose up Theudas, boasting himself to be somebody; to whom a number of men, about four hundred, joined themselves: who was slain; and all, as many as obeyed him, were scattered, and brought to nought.
>
> After this man rose up Judas of Galilee in the days of the taxing, and drew away much people after him: he also perished; and all, even as many as obeyed him, were dispersed.
>
> And now I say unto you, Refrain from these men, and let them alone: for if this counsel or this work be of men, it will come to nought:
>
> But if it be of God, ye cannot overthrow it; lest haply ye be found even to fight against God.
>
> And to him they agreed: and when they had called the apostles, and beaten them, they com-

manded that they should not speak in the name of Jesus, and let them go. (Acts 5:34–40.)

Did Gamaliel have any spiritual promptings which caused him to call for fair play for the Apostles? Did he later affiliate with the Church of Jesus Christ? We do not now know. But the wisdom of Gamaliel was surely significant: "Refrain from these men, and let them alone: for if this counsel or this work be of men, it will come to nought: but if it be of God, ye cannot overthrow it; lest haply ye be found even to fight against God."

Significantly, Gamaliel named two other leaders. Theudas had had about four hundred followers and was slain. Theudas's followers were scattered and "brought to nought." There was apparently a "Judas of Galilee" who drew many people away after him. He also perished and his followers were dispersed. Jesus' followers were scattered "like sheep" after he was slain (see Mark 14:27). But instead of being "brought to nought" Jesus' work grew, just as Gamaliel had indicated it would do "if it be of God."

Just as there were men like Theudas and Judas of Galilee who made it more difficult in a way for some to recognize who Jesus of Nazareth really was, so there were others in the time of Joseph Smith whose religious movements, by and large, came to naught.

Often in the history of God's work individuals who had a sense of fair play have been most helpful, whether Colonel Kane or Gamaliel or the intriguing town clerk of Ephesus (see Acts 19:23–41). Apparently in that last-named circumstance, the worshipers of Diana raised a tumult against Paul, chanting for the space of two hours saying, "Great is Diana of the Ephesians."

An unnamed town clerk stepped forward to appease the people, urging them "to be quiet, and to do nothing rashly." The silver makers, who feared for the future of their craft, since they made silver shrines for Diana, had a vested interest. It was the town clerk, however, who pointed out that Paul and his followers "are neither robbers of churches, nor yet blasphemers of your goddess." Therefore, reasoned the town clerk, if Demetrius, a leader among the silversmiths, had "a matter against any man, the law is open, and there are deputies; let them implead one another." The town clerk urged all to let matters "be determined in the lawful assembly" but not by a mob, warning that they were "in danger to be called in question for this day's uproar, there being no cause whereby we may give an account of this concourse. And when he had thus spoken, he dismissed the assembly" (Acts 19:37–41).

The Home Secretary in Britain assisted missionaries of The Church of Jesus Christ of Latter-day Saints when there were members of Parliament who would have prohibited them from proselyting. At least seven times (in 1910 and 1911) there were exchanges in Parliament when some urged steps to prevent meetings of Church members in Britain, so they could not "spread their views in this country." A very young Home Secretary—the youngest, in fact, to serve since Peel—parried pressing parliamentarians. His name was Winston Churchill. He said, "I have no power to prevent the holding of such meetings as long as they are held in conformity with the law."

It was a time of serious social unrest and there was violence in the mines. Churchill was even being accused of making prison life too uncomfortable. Though perhaps a reluctant and disapproving protector, Churchill stood his ground because "there is very wide divergence of opinion in this country . . ." and Churchill had not "so far discovered any ground for legislative action" in the Mormon matter. In late

1911, he became the First Lord of the Admiralty. His successor in the Home Office wrote a letter in 1914 confirming that "extensive enquiries . . . did not reveal any grounds for legislative action." (Arthur L. Beeley, *A Summary Statement of the Investigation Made by the British Government of the "Mormon" Question in England,* p. 13.)

As to their salvational or developmental worth, there is no democracy among the verses of holy writ. Some verses are useful, while others are supernal.

Moroni's abridgement of the writings of Ether, for instance, gives us lineage history such as in this verse, compressing five generations:

> And he begat Heth, and Heth lived in captivity all his days. And Heth begat Aaron, and Aaron dwelt in captivity all his days; and he begat Amnigaddah, and Amnigaddah also dwelt in captivity all his days; and he begat Coriantum, and Coriantum dwelt in captivity all his days; and he begat Com. (Ether 10:31.)

However, the Book of Ether in addition to some such data on succession provides us with much inspiration, including these stern but realistic lines concerning our personal development:

> And if men come unto me I will show unto them their weakness. I give unto men weakness that they may be humble; and my grace is sufficient for all men that humble themselves before me; for if they humble themselves before me, and have faith in me, then will I make weak things become strong unto them. (Ether 12:27.)

Moreover, the scriptures remind us that our time in the mortal schoolhouse is so fleeting, "The time passed away with us, and also our lives passed away like as it were unto us a dream . . ." (Jacob 7:28). How well we use the precious time alloted to us makes all the difference, because this life is "a time to prepare to meet God" (Alma 12:24).

There is also to be found and appreciated in the searching of the scriptures the several levels of meaning that can be uncovered in certain verses:

> O, then, my beloved brethren, come unto the Lord, the Holy One. Remember that his paths are righteous. Behold, the way for man is narrow, but it lieth in a straight course before him, and the keeper of the gate is the Holy One of Israel; and he employeth no servant there; and there is none other way save it be by the gate; for he cannot be deceived, for the Lord God is his name. (2 Nephi 9:41.)

Additionally, in the Joseph Smith Translation the serious searcher will discover heretofore hidden meaning in certain verses:

> And the Lord said unto Moses, Hew thee two other tables of stone, like unto the first, and I will write upon them also, the words of the law, according as they were written at the first on the tables which thou brakest; but it shall not be according to the first, for I will take away the priesthood out of their midst; therefore my holy order, and the ordinances thereof, shall not go before them; for my presence shall not go up in their midst, lest I destroy them (JST Exodus 34:1).

Clearly, temple-related blessings were among the things not given to ancient Israel when God's people were given a lesser law and lesser blessings.

Another example of scriptures which are foretelling (but more in an intriguing than in a delineating way) is this verse:

> That the kingdoms of this world may be constrained to acknowledge that the kingdom of Zion is in very deed the kingdom of our God and his Christ; there-

fore, let us become subject unto her laws (D&C
105:32).

This verse suggests a time when there will be some
public acknowledgement concerning the Kingdom of
Zion. Some will apparently be willing to become subject to the laws of Zion and to acknowledge that Zion
represents "the kingdom of our God and his Christ."
This intriguing verse stands alone, much as does an intriguing verse in Zechariah:

> And one shall say unto him, What are these wounds
> in thine hands? Then he shall answer, Those with
> which I was wounded in the house of my friends.
> (Zechariah 13:6.)

In the case of this verse in Zechariah, however, we
have amplifying modern revelation:

> And then shall the Jews look upon me and say: What
> are these wounds in thine hands and in thy feet?
>   Then shall they know that I am the Lord; for I
> will say unto them: These wounds are the wounds
> with which I was wounded in the house of my
> friends. I am he who was lifted up. I am Jesus that
> was crucified. I am the Son of God.
>   And then shall they weep because of their iniqui-
> ties; then shall they lament because they persecuted
> their king. (D&C 45:51–53.)

But what of the verse in section 105 of the Doctrine
and Covenants?

As well as that in D&C 45:67–69, we have this interesting comment from John Taylor:

> Those who will not take up their sword to fight
> against their neighbor must needs flee to Zion for
> safety. And they will come, saying, We do not know
> anything of the principles of your religion, but we
> perceive that you are an honest community; you ad-
> minister justice and righteousness, and we want to
> live with you and receive the protection of your

laws, but as for your religion we will talk about that some other time. Will we protect such people? Yes, all honorable men. (*Journal of Discourses* 21:8.)

This is a prophecy of a remarkable circumstance yet to come to pass, whether it is millennial or premillennial. In either case it is an example of another one of those foretelling jewels which lie imbedded in the books of scripture for those who have eyes to see. The later point of transition will finally be reached, in any event, as John the Revelator declared.

And the seventh angel sounded; and there were great voices in heaven, saying, The kingdoms of this world are become the kingdoms of our Lord, and of his Christ; and he shall reign for ever and ever (Revelation 11:15).

A parallel and confirming revelation has come in our time:

And thus, with the sword and by bloodshed the inhabitants of the earth shall mourn; and with famine, and plague, and earthquake, and the thunder of heaven, and the fierce and vivid lightning also, shall the inhabitants of the earth be made to feel the wrath, and indignation, and chastening hand of an Almighty God, until the consumption decreed hath made a full end of all nations (D&C 87:6).

We understand, of course, that there will be many nonmembers of the Church living during the Millennium, but there will be a clear willingness by all the good and decent men and women of all the races, creeds, and cultures to abide by a terrestrial law.

In the millennium men will have the privilege of being Presbyterians, Methodists or Infidels, but they will not have the privilege of treating the name and character of Deity as they have done heretofore (Brigham Young, *Journal of Discourses* 12:274).

Some members of the Church have an erroneous
idea that when the millennium comes all of the
people are going to be swept off the earth except
righteous members of the Church. That is not so.
There will be millions of people, Catholics, Protes-
tants, agnostics, Mohammedans, people of all
classes, and of all beliefs, still permitted to remain
upon the face of the earth, but they will be those
who have lived clean lives, those who have been
free from wickedness and corruption. All who
belong, by virtue of their good lives, to the terrestrial order, as well as those who have kept the celes-
tial law, will remain upon the face of the earth
during the millennium. (Joseph Fielding Smith,
Doctrines of Salvation [Bookcraft, 1954] 1:86.)

Thus, as we search the scriptures and the words of
living prophets, not only do we see how the scriptures
testify of Christ. Also in this searching we very often
find episodes and parallels to give us precious perspective in these days which are our days and also glimpses
of a glorious future.

"The Indignation of the Lord"

(D&C 97:24)

It is customary, even understandable, when we read of God's indignation and anger to think of it in terms of an angry mortal father and to not ponder it much more. Some even mutter about Old Testament "tribalism," mistakenly thinking of God as being personally piqued or offended at some human act of wickedness or stupidity because He has told us to behave otherwise. This is erroneous, bumper-sticker theology. Simply because we are, so often, angry at a wrong done to us, we assume the same about God's anger.

Several scriptures illustrate some of the familiar expressions which are often wrongly construed as above. These verses are but two examples:

> Even all nations shall say, Wherefore hath the Lord done thus unto this land? what meaneth the heat of this great anger?

Then men shall say, Because they have forsaken the covenant of the Lord God of their fathers, which he made with them when he brought them forth out of the land of Egypt:

For they went and served other gods, and worshipped them, gods whom they knew not, and whom he had not given unto them:

And the anger of the Lord was kindled against this land, to bring upon it all the curses that are written in this book:

And the Lord rooted them out of their land in anger, and in wrath, and in great indignation, and cast them into another land, as it is this day. (Deuteronomy 29:24–28.)

Therefore thus saith the Lord God; Behold, mine anger and my fury shall be poured out upon this place, upon man, and upon beast, and upon the trees of the field, and upon the fruit of the ground; and it shall burn, and shall not be quenched (Jeremiah 7:20).

Instead, we should think of God in terms of His divine attributes, for He is perfect in His love, mercy, and compassion—as well as in His justice. Only then can we begin to understand *why* His anger is kindled and to appreciate the loving concern which underlies His wrath. God's love for us is perfect, and His desire for our happiness is so deep that when His anger is kindled this signals much more than we realize. Our God is not preoccupied with other concerns, nor is His ego offended, as are ours. Such narrow views of Him do an injustice to God who is perfect in His justice.

While God's love is pure and perfect, Henry Fairlie has written that our mortal anger is often perverted love, for instance, "the love of justice perverted into the desire for revenge" (*The Seven Deadly Sins Today*, p. 108). God's indignation is quite a different matter.

God's anger is kindled not because we have harmed him but because we have harmed ourselves. We are His children and He is a perfect Father. He does not want us, for instance, to take His name in vain, but this.is because of what happens to us when we do. Our profanity cannot diminish from His Godhood, His love, His omnipotence, or His omniscience. But our profanity does damage us and can damage us profoundly.

We read, for instance, that He experiences a deep, divine disappointment in us when we are ungrateful and when we are unwilling to confess God's hand in all things. (D&C 59:21.) But it is because of what our sustained ingratitude does to us, not to Him. Failure to see His hand in human affairs in bringing to pass His eternal purposes and plans in the world (at the same time leaving us to exercise our free agency) is a fatal misreading of life. It also represents a profound spur to selfishness and self-centeredness. It is these faults which lead to the celebration of the appetites rather than of spiritual things. And God knows perfectly what the end results of such trends are so far as human misery is concerned. It is our true happiness which He desires for us, His children, and "wickedness never was happiness" (Alma 41:10).

God is our Father. He knows better than we what we have the power to become. He would not be a true Father God if He were content with us just as we are, because He knows what we have the possibilities to become. Even so, He has said to us, "Nevertheless, thou mayest choose for thyself" (Moses 3:17).

We see an example of His divine disappointment in an episode early in Moses' spiritual career, when Moses worried that he was not eloquent, that he was slow of speech and slow of tongue (see Exodus 4:10). The Lord remonstrated with him, even promising Moses that He would "teach thee what thou shalt say" (verse 12). This was not enough, hence Aaron's role. Thus we see in a very early scriptural episode a failure to trust in the Lord and a settling for something less. God's indignation was over what might have been.

Surely ancient Israel's tendency to follow other gods provoked the Lord to anger, but we must be careful not to look at that anger through finite mortal eyes. After all, what is to be said of a people who prefer to worship dumb idols and gods of wood and stone? Especially after so many miracles had been performed by the real Father-God for them? Hence Isaiah spoke about God's "indignation toward his enemies" (Isaiah 66:14). Those who prevent human happiness include those who traffic in drugs, narcotics, and child pornography. Because God loves His children and He is our friend, He is angry at our enemies and those foolish and misery-producing acts inculcated by our enemies.

If true but imperfect friends feel that way, would not a perfect Heavenly Father so feel, only much more deeply?

There is an immensely important insight in this episode concerning our healing Savior:

And he entered again into the synagogue; and there was a man there which had a withered hand.

And they watched him, whether he would heal him on the sabbath day; that they might accuse him.

And he saith unto the man which had the withered hand, Stand forth.

And he saith unto them, Is it lawful to do good on the sabbath days, or to do evil? to save life, or to kill? But they held their peace.

And when *he* had *looked round about on them with anger, being grieved for the hardness of their hearts,* he saith unto the man, Stretch forth thine hand. And he stretched it out: and his hand was restored whole as the other. (Mark 3:1–5, italics added.)

Jesus' indignation was over "the hardness of their hearts," over their inability to see how appropriate a healing on the Sabbath day was, especially for a man who had endured a withered hand for so many Sabbaths before.

How contorted and distorted the thinking was of those who were critical of Jesus for violating the Sabbath day! After all, He was Lord of the Sabbath, and they clearly misunderstood the purpose of the Sabbath. Jesus' critics were, in effect, denying the value of a miracle just performed. However, should not man be entitled to do "good" on the Sabbath as well as on any other day?

As Paul wrote, the wrath of God is aroused against all ungodliness (Romans 1:18). The gross sexual immorality afflicting some of the Ephesians was, as Paul wrote, the cause of "the wrath of God upon the children of disobedience" (Ephesians 5:6). Who knows better than our Father and His Son Jesus Christ what the long-term, deep, and miserable consequences of gross sexual immorality are?

Those who wrongly and grossly celebrate their capacity to feel, lose their God-given capacity to feel. The beautiful world around them thereafter goes unseen and unappreciated, because their concerns are focused on a single but shrinking plane of action. The desensitization which follows sexual immorality produces all sorts of social consequences for the individual, his or her victims, and the family, as well as society. In the case of Sodom and Gomorrah in a time of gross sexual immorality, they neglected their poor and needy (Ezekiel 16:49).

Then there are the lamentable inward consequences, which God well knows. Jacob wrote about these in another time of gross sexual immorality, when children lost respect for their fathers, when "many hearts died, pierced with deep wounds" (Jacob 2:35). How much misery permeated these families we know not, but it would have been considerable.

Since wickedness never was happiness, when wickedness is rife God's indignation is understandably ripe (see D&C 29:17).

His indignation is likewise kindled when we hide our talents (D&C 60:2). Our service to our neighbor is thus diminished, and his and our happiness lessened.

We must remember, too, that we worship a loving Father in Heaven who is anxious to give us even further gifts and spiritual confirmations. But His perfectly giving nature cannot operate under certain conditions.

> Yea, signs come by faith, unto mighty works, for without faith no man pleaseth God; and with whom God is angry he is not well pleased; wherefore, unto such he showeth no signs, only in wrath unto their condemnation (D&C 63:11).

The sparks are struck as His desire to give to us grinds against our inability and unwillingness to receive.

God's indignation is checked by His perfect love, mercy, and compassion. Our own anger is usually not. No wonder Paul counseled us not to be easily provoked (1 Corinthians 13:5). No wonder parents are counseled not to provoke their children to anger (Colossians 3:21). Bishops are counseled in similar terms (Titus 1:7).

Thus divine anger is rich in its redemptiveness, and it rests on love; it is a far different thing than the pique and petulance we know and display on our mortal scale. Of course, righteous indignation is possible for us. It too is commendable when it is in check through love and compassion and when it occurs by showing increased love after deserved and inspired reproof (D&C 121:43).

In the tutoring and the developing of that remarkable man, Enoch, we also see how his indignation came to mirror those considerations which underlie the Lord's indignation. Given some extensive understanding through visions of the human future, tender Enoch wept when he viewed how the "residue of the people" would not respond to the gospel of Jesus Christ (Moses 7:28). Enoch even asked the Lord how it was that the Lord "canst weep" over people on this planet amid the vastness of His creations, especially when there may be "millions of earths like this" (verses 29–30).

The Lord's response is very instructive. He recounted to Enoch that man was created and given certain knowledge, intelligence, and also agency (verse 32). That mankind also were given special commandments that "they should love one another, and that they should choose me, their Father; but behold, they are without affection, and they hate their own blood" (verse 33). For those reasons, the Lord indicates, "the fire of mine indignation is kindled against them." Hence the flood at the time of Noah. A Father perfect in love and affection was stirred by man's lack of affection, even man's lack of love for "their own blood."

It is particularly poignant that those to whom the Lord then referred were apparently more wicked than any of the people "among all the workmanship of mine hands" (verse 36). These men and women would choose Satan to be their father and thus "misery shall be their doom." Hence came the final answer to Enoch's question: "The whole heavens shall weep over them, even all the workmanship of mine hands;

wherefore, should not the heavens weep, seeing these shall suffer?" (verse 37). It is very, very significant that the heavens wept because "these shall suffer." Because, they having chosen Satan, misery was to be their lot. Yet they were their Father's spirit children!

How much this tells us, especially about the purposeful and perfect love of a Father whose ceaseless work is "to bring to pass the immortality and eternal life of man"! (Moses 1:39)

Even then, as we read, Enoch was told that a Redeemer, Jesus Christ, was to be sent among the children of men. Still later, even among those who rejected Jesus, there would be missionary work done in the spirit world (see D&C 138).

It is in the presence of these reassurances and this perspective that the Lord "told Enoch all the doings of the children of men." Enoch came to look "upon their wickedness, and their misery, and wept and stretched forth his arms, and his heart swelled wide as eternity; and his bowels yearned; and all eternity shook" (Moses 7:41). Thus those tutored by the Lord become more and more like Him, including in the qualities of empathy and indignation.

As tenderly and tellingly as Enoch saw the Flood and the destruction of the wicked, "he had bitterness of soul, and wept over his brethren, and said unto the heavens: I will refuse to be comforted; but the Lord said unto Enoch: Lift up your heart, and be glad; and look" (Moses 7:44). Then Enoch was treated with a vision of that which would happen with the coming of Jesus Christ and His mortal ministry and subsequent events.

> And the Lord showed Enoch all things, even unto the end of the world; and he saw the day of the righteous, the hour of their redemption, and received a fulness of joy (Moses 7:67).

It is the Lord's hand in all things that we are to confess and make allowance for. Those who do not believe in God or in the meaning and purpose of life and
in His plan of salvation simply cannot do this.

Very significantly, Enoch went on to help perfect
the City of Enoch and its righteous inhabitants, a happy
people who were "of one heart and one mind" (Moses
7:18). It is the only time in human history when a righteous people did not relapse. Significantly too, all
this was accomplished under the leadership of an ex-
panded Enoch who, when he had been called, asked
why he had been called—because I "am but a lad, and
all the people hate me; for I am slow of speech" (Moses
6:31).

Yet he trusted in the Lord, and the Lord unfolded
Enoch's possibilities and talents in a most remarkable
way.

Thus as we search the scriptures our understanding
in all matters can be deepened, our perceptivity enlarged, and our adoration of our Father in Heaven and
His only begotten Son, Jesus Christ, immeasurably enhanced—even as concerns the anger and the indignation of God!

The fact is that a loving Father watches over His
children and is deeply concerned with our suffering
and with our misery, whether that suffering is a result
of pride or pornography, drugs or devil worship, ag-
gression or perversion, or the worship of false gods.

Being a loving Father, though deeply devoted to
our free agency, there are times in human history when
He simply could not continue to send spirits to this
earth who would have had virtually no chance. This
was the case with Sodom and Gomorrah and the cities
of the plains.

Hence it was better to destroy a few individuals,
than to entail misery on many. And hence the in-

habitants of the old world and of the cities of Sodom and Gomorrah were destroyed, because it was better for them to die, and thus be deprived of their agency, which they abused, than entail so much misery on their posterity, and bring ruin upon millions of unborn persons. (John Taylor, *The Government of God* [Liverpool: S.W. Richards, 1852], p. 53.)

If we were like the people before the flood, full of violence and oppression; or if we, like the Sodomites or Canaanites, were full of all manner of lawless abominations, holding promiscuous intercourse with the other sex, and stooping to a level with the brute creation, and predisposing our children, by every means in our power, to be fully given to strange and unnatural lusts, appetites, and passions, would it not be a mercy to cut us off, root and branch, and thus put an end to our increase upon the earth? You will all say it would. The spirits in heaven would thank God for preventing them from being born into the world under such circumstances. (Parley P. Pratt, *Journal of Discourses* 1:259.)

Another time in human history when such degradation was reached was the time preceding the Flood, in which Noah and others were spared. Similarly there were conditions in the Nephite society when people were "without civilization," "without order," "without mercy," were "strong in their perversions," and were "past feeling." (Moroni chapter 9.)

Likewise, the Lord has indicated that for the sake of the elect He will shorten the days before the Second Coming, when human suffering will be intense.

In every instance, social ills are self-induced—it is not God but human misuse of the agency God has given us which causes our misery and suffering. He would clearly have it otherwise.

Thus neither God nor His Church nor His leaders can look with indifference upon those things which bring so much human misery and suffering. Genuine and righteous indignation, however, is always redemptive. Indeed such indignation, properly heeded, can reduce human misery now and the shame which will otherwise be present on that distant day. A special circumstance of final judgment will come when, in the words of Alma (Alma 12:15),

> we must come forth and stand before him in his glory, and in his power, and in his might, majesty, and dominion, and acknowledge to our everlasting shame that all his judgments are just; that he is just in all his works, and that he is merciful unto the children of men, and that he has all power to save every man that believeth on his name and bringeth forth fruit meet for repentance.

SERMON NUMBER NINE

"A Peculiar People"
(1 Peter 2:9)

Though this book seeks to encourage God's chosen people—that is, those who have chosen to become so—ever to be remembered is the fact that God is "no respecter of persons" (see Acts 10:34; 17:26; Romans 2:11; 1 Nephi 17:35; D&C 1:35). He is the Father of us all. But just as through His Beloved Son all mankind will be resurrected, so also by chosen peoples God seeks further to redeem all other people, whose present or past unawareness of His work matters little in this respect. After all, long ago the bounds of the various nations and habitations were fixed by God (see Acts 17:26; Deuteronomy 32:8).

God's plan of salvation took into account in advance all that a perfect plan would require.

Moreover, given God's deep commitment to human agency, the Lord, without approving of it, allows for human stupidity. Mortal shortfalls were taken into account in God's unfolding plan of salvation. For instance, the provincial, Ptolemaic view of the earth prevailed for centuries until overturned by the Copernican view when the earth was no longer mistakenly thought to be the center of the universe.

Now, in our age of seeming enlightenment we too must be careful about our own forms of provincialism. For example, the atoning mission of Jesus on this planet *may* affect others elsewhere (see D&C 88: 46–61; 76:24).

Yet as important as the Lord's chosen people have been, in the secular sweep of history—except for an occasional and acknowledging nod from and occasional brushes with world class figures (Sheba, Cyrus, Nebuchadnezzar, and so on)—the Lord's people throughout the centuries have gone quietly about their tasks content with their seeming obscurity.

Yes, Winston Churchill once courageously defended Britain's religious tolerance on the floor of Parliament, so that the Mormon missionaries might continue their work.

Yes, General George S. Patton had some favorable comments to make about one of the Twelve whom he met in Mexico: "Very interesting and educated." Yet with a candor confirming the wisdom of his choice of a military career over that of a diplomatic career, Patton also wrote: "It seems strange that such a smart man could be a leader in such a fool religion" (p. 360, *The Patton Papers 1885–1940,* Martin Blumenson). Patton later went on to his great battles. Like the ancient Greeks as they viewed Christianity, Patton saw the expression of Latter-day Christianity as "foolishness" (1 Corinthians 1:18–23). Patton's mind had apparently been adversely influenced by a 1903 anti-Church book of fiction.

President Van Buren may have had a few uncomfortable moments with the Prophet Joseph, whose cause he described as just but for whom he said he could do nothing. Like Pilate with his eyes on Rome, Van Buren had his own Missouri.

Nevertheless God's work has gone on quietly and obscurely. After all, the resurrected Jesus did not triumphantly visit the Sanhedrin, Caiaphas, Herod, or Pilate. Rather, His resurrected Presence blessed bands of believers in obscure Bethany and, later, in Bountiful.

Christian verity issues from obscurity. It is the truth, not its host turf, that matters!

Peter, as a fisherman, was in an excellent position to give this caveat to those who are chosen of God, for he wrote that converts are "newborn babes [in Christ] . . . disallowed indeed of men, but chosen of God, and precious" (1 Peter 2:1–4). Surely Peter knew what it was to be "disallowed indeed of men." Those "in the know" in his time regarded him as unlearned and "ignorant" (Acts 4:13). It was Peter who boldly characterized those whom God had chosen.

> But ye are a chosen generation, a royal priesthood, an holy nation, a peculiar people; that ye should shew forth the praises of him who hath called you out of darkness into his marvellous light (1 Peter 2:9).

Peculiar, of course, in the Greek rendition should denote not eccentricity but "purchased, preserved, treasured, rare." "Purchased" denotes being "bought" and freed by Jesus' atonement.

Centuries before, the Lord remarked of His covenant people that He had "chosen [them] to be a special people" (Deuteronomy 7:6).

But any exclusivity is quickly pervaded and overwhelmed by a sense of sobering duty. Even so, the Lord said to ancient Israel, "You only have I known of all the families of the earth" (Amos 3:2).

Furthermore, where "much is given much is required" (D&C 82:3). Note that the word is not *expected* but *required*. For any people favored of God (see 2 Nephi 1:19), it is obligatory for them to favor God's way of life and to keep His stern but sweet commandments. Thus they can then be a much-needed "light unto the Gentiles" (D&C 86:11). Ways in which they are to be peculiar will include their purity (see D&C 100:16), as this quality, too, comprises a standard for other people (see D&C 115:5).

It is through those who have such extra blessings that "all families of the earth [will] be blessed" (Genesis 12:3). The chosen people are to be much less caught up in the cares of the world as they seek "first to build up the kingdom of God, and to establish his righteousness" (JST Matthew 6:38).

The Lord's chosen are also not to be barren but are to "bring forth fruit" (John 15:16); not only in terms of missionary work but also the visible fruits of gospel living. This is to be achieved even though the persons and the people thus chosen are to live amid perverse nations as wheat among the tares. (Philippians 2:15.) Such Saints are to eschew secular power and instead are to be "armed with righteousness" (1 Nephi 14:14). They are, likewise, to "bring to pass the gathering of mine elect" (D&C 29:7).

Again, "of him unto whom much is given much is required" (D&C 82:3), including the requirement that "Zion must increase in beauty, and in holiness" (D&C 82:14).

One cannot review scriptures such as the foregoing without a duality of feelings: feelings of *responsibility* toward God and feelings regarding His *generosity extended* to us.

Clearly, in this respect the dispensation of the fulness of times is different from all the others. The stone cut out of the mountain without hands, as foreseen by Daniel (Daniel 2:34, 44), is to grow until one day it will fill the earth. The Church is thus to come forth out of the wilderness and out of obscurity (see D&C 1:30; 5:14). Thus with the ending of obscurity and the simultaneous increase in visibility, disciples in the last days will experience both special opportunities and special challenges.

Faithful Latter-day disciples, however, were—men and women alike—carefully chosen and prepared long, long ago:

> And this is the manner after which they were ordained—being called and prepared from the foundation of the world according to the foreknowledge of God, on account of their exceeding faith and good works; in the first place being left to choose good or evil; therefore they having chosen good, and exercising exceeding great faith, are called with a holy calling, yea, with that holy calling which was prepared with, and according to, a preparatory redemption for such (Alma 13:3).

> Now the Lord had shown unto me, Abraham, the intelligences that were organized before the world was; and among all these there were many of the noble and great ones;
> And God saw these souls that they were good, and he stood in the midst of them, and he said: These I will make my rulers; for he stood among those that were spirits, and he saw that they were good; and he said unto me Abraham, thou art one of them; thou wast chosen before thou wast born. (Abraham 3:22, 23.)

> According as he hath chosen us in him before the foundation of the world, that we should be holy and without blame before him in love (Ephesians 1:4).

> Elect according to the foreknowledge of God the Father, through sanctification of the Spirit, unto obedience and sprinkling of the blood of Jesus Christ: Grace unto you, and peace, be multiplied (1 Peter 1:2).

The Prophet Joseph Smith, and my father, Hyrum
Smith, Brigham Young, John Taylor, Wilford Wood-
ruff, and other choice spirits who were reserved to
come forth in the fulness of times to take part in
laying the foundations of the great latter-day work,

Including the building of the temples and the
performance of ordinances therein for the redemption of the dead, were also in the spirit world.

I observed that they were also among the noble
and great ones who were chosen in the beginning to
be rulers in the Church of God.

Even before they were born, they, with many
others, received their first lessons in the world of
spirits and were prepared to come forth in the due
time of the Lord to labor in his vineyard for the salvation of the souls of men. (D&C 138:53–56.)

Pondering such verses as these evokes humble
gratitude but also wonderment. They can freshen and
stiffen one's determination to rise to his or her moment
in history and to be *in* the world but not *of* it.

Words like "chosen" and "prepared" and "received their first lessons in the world of spirits" brace
us as we are now being further prepared and are now
receiving our second lessons in the second estate.

As the human scene attests, there is ample need for
the contributions to mankind of all who are "chosen
. . . to be a special people." Their meekness will drain
off the considerations of ego. Their love can enclose
the absolute truths they bear and would share with
their fellowmen. The eloquence of their example will
compensate for any slowness of speech.

The only aristocracy the world has nothing to fear
from is an aristocracy of Saints, for their access to the
powers of heaven is predicated upon their personal
righteousness. And their imperfections are eroded,
albeit slowly, in their striving to become like their
King.

Index

— V —

Values, decline of, 29–31
Van Buren, Martin, 95–96
Vengeance, 36

— W —

War, chemical, 36
  germ, 36
  nuclear, 32–36
Wars, 29, 31, 66–68
Wickedness, 54–64
Wordsworth, William, 12
World problems, 27–39

World War I, 66, 67
Worldliness, 10–16, 62

— Y —

Young, Brigham, on faith, 6, 58
  on Joseph Smith, 50
  on Millennium, 81
Youth, 2

— Z —

Zechariah, 80
Zion, Kingdom of, 79–80